US Government Core Concepts Series

From the Constitution to Congress: The Foundations of Authority, Representation & Governance in the United States

Peter Caldwell

TME Press email: support@tme.net

Introduction

In May 1787, fifty-five men gathered in a room in Philadelphia and did something radical. They nailed the windows shut. Despite the stifling summer heat, they chose secrecy over comfort. They knew that if word of their debates leaked too early, the fragile union of thirteen states might collapse before a single page was signed. These men were going beyond writing a legal document; they were designing an experiment in human nature. They wanted to see if a people could govern themselves without a king, a dictator, or a hereditary elite. That experiment became the United States Constitution, a document that continues to guide the most complex democracy on Earth.

Understanding how this government works isn't just a task for students or lawyers. It's a necessity for anyone who wants to participate in the life of the nation. The rules written over two centuries ago, and the ways we have adapted them since, determine how your taxes are spent, how your rights are protected, and how your voice is heard in Washington. This book serves as your roadmap through those rules. It strips away the academic jargon to show you the mechanical heart of American governance.

The Value of This Guide

Most people recognize the names of the three branches of government, yet explaining how they actually check one another isn't easy for most. This book fills that gap. You'll find a factual exploration of the authority that drives our country. We examine the specific powers granted to each branch and the limits that keep them in line. You will gain a concrete understanding of why the system often feels slow or frustrating, and why the Founders intended it to be exactly that way.

The value of this knowledge becomes clear the moment you turn on the news or read a political headline. When you understand the difference between an enumerated power and an implied one, or the reality of how a committee markup actually changes a law, you can see past the partisan noise. You'll be able to judge for yourself whether a president is overstepping their authority or if Congress is failing to exercise its constitutional duties. This book gives you the objective criteria to be an informed observer and a more effective citizen.

How This Book Is Structured

We have organized this series to follow the logical arc of the American story. We begin with the origins. Chapter 1 explores the deep roots of our system, from English common law to the Enlightenment philosophies that gave the Founders their intellectual muscle. You'll see that the Revolution wasn't just a tax revolt; it was a fundamental argument about the nature of rights.

Chapter 2 takes you inside that hot room in Philadelphia. We break down the competing interests of the delegates and the compromises that saved the convention from collapse. Following that, Chapter 3 provides an article-by-article tour of the

Constitution itself. We look at the preamble and the basic structure that holds the entire federal government together.

Because the Constitution almost failed to pass, Chapter 4 focuses on the ratification battle and the birth of the Bill of Rights. This section is vital for understanding why we have specific protections for speech, religion, and the accused. From there, we move into the structural reality of the nation. Chapter 5 explains federalism, the often-messy division of power between the states and the national government. Chapter 6 then goes into the separation of powers, showing you the "Madisonian" theory that uses ambition to counteract ambition.

The middle of the book focuses on the "first branch" of government: Congress. Across Chapters 7 through 11, we look at everything from how elections work to how a bill actually survives the legislative process. You'll learn about the committee system, the power of the purse, and the non-legislative authorities like impeachment and oversight.

We then shift our focus to the executive and judicial branches. Chapter 12 examines the presidency and the vast federal bureaucracy that carries out the law. Chapter 13 explores the federal courts and the different ways judges interpret the Constitution. We close the book by looking at the results of this system in practice. Chapter 14 covers civil liberties and rights, while Chapter 15 looks at the external influences of parties and lobbyists. Finally, Chapter 16 addresses the contemporary challenges facing our government today, from polarization to gridlock.

Practical Methods for Learning

We have designed this book to be as clear and scannable as possible. You'll notice that chapters include summary tables. These organize complex information (like the differences between the Virginia and New Jersey plans or the types of congressional committees) into a format you can digest at a glance. From the early 1600s to today, we cover more than 400 years of history with enough depth to build real understanding while keeping the material manageable enough to complete. We don't want you to get lost in walls of text; we want you to see the structure of the ideas immediately.

Each chapter concludes with a specific, thought-provoking question. They're designed to make you think about how the concepts you just read apply to the real world. To help you compare your own thinking, we have provided example answers for every one of these questions. You can find these answers located right after the conclusion at the back of the book.

A Realistic Approach

This isn't a book of political theory or idealism. It's a book about how things work in the real world. We treat the federal bureaucracy as a complex machine and the legislative process as a grueling competition. You won't find moralizing or partisan opinions here. Our goal is to provide you with the facts so you can reach your own conclusions about the health and future of the American republic.

The American government is a massive, interlocking system of rules, traditions, and laws. It can feel overwhelming, but it's ultimately a human creation. It was built by people who were worried about the same things we worry about today: safety, freedom, and the fair exercise of power. Learning the foundations of this system, you are doing more than just studying history; you are learning how to use the most important instrument ever created for self-government.

As you move through these chapters, try to look for the patterns. Notice how often the same tensions reappear. The struggle between state and federal power that began in 1787 is the same struggle we see in modern court cases about healthcare or the environment.

The people, fashion, and technologies change over time, but a lot of the same things happen repeatedly throughout history for many of the same reasons. The debate over executive power that concerned the Anti-Federalists is the same one we have every time a president issues a new executive order. These are the recurring themes of the American story.

We've kept the language simple and friendly because these ideas belong to everyone. You don't need a doctorate in political science to understand the Supremacy Clause or the Electoral College. You simply need a clear explanation and a bit of curiosity. This book provides the explanation; your curiosity will do the rest.

Welcome to the foundations of American authority. Whether you're reading this to prepare for a class or simply to be a better-informed citizen or voter, you are taking a vital step. Knowledge of the system is the only way to be sure that the "experiment" the Founders started in that locked room continues to function for the next generation. It's a heavy responsibility, but it's one we all share. Let's begin.

Overview

Chapter 1: Origins of American Government

- Colonial governance and self-rule traditions
- English common law inheritance
- Enlightenment political philosophy
- Grievances under British rule
- The Declaration of Independence
- Articles of Confederation and their failures

Chapter 2: The Constitutional Convention

- Delegates and their competing interests
- The Virginia Plan
- The New Jersey Plan
- The Great Compromise
- The Three-Fifths Compromise

Chapter 3: Structure and Text of the Constitution

- The Preamble and its purpose
- Article-by-article overview
- Enumerated powers
- Implied powers

Chapter 4: Ratification and the Bill of Rights

- Federalist arguments
- Anti-Federalist objections
- State ratifying conventions
- The first ten amendments
- Incorporation against the states
- Subsequent constitutional amendments

Chapter 5: Federalism and the Division of Power

- Dual federalism
- Cooperative federalism

- Reserved powers of the states
- Concurrent powers
- The Supremacy Clause

Chapter 6: Separation of Powers and Checks and Balances

- Madisonian theory of factions
- Legislative checks on the executive
- Executive checks on the legislature
- Judicial review
- Veto and override mechanisms

Chapter 7: The Legislative Branch

- Bicameralism and its rationale
- House of Representatives composition
- Senate composition
- Qualifications and terms of office
- Constitutional powers of Congress
- Enumerated versus implied authority

Chapter 8: Congressional Elections and Representation

- Apportionment and reapportionment
- Redistricting and gerrymandering
- Single-member districts
- Incumbency advantage

Chapter 9: How Congress Organizes Itself

- Party leadership in the House
- Party leadership in the Senate
- The committee system
- Standing, select, and joint committees
- Caucuses and conferences

Chapter 10: The Legislative Process

- Bill introduction and sponsorship
- Committee markup and hearings
- Floor debate and amendment

- Cloture and the filibuster
- Conference committees
- Presidential signature and veto

Chapter 11: Congressional Powers Beyond Lawmaking

- The power of the purse
- Oversight and investigation
- Impeachment authority
- Treaty ratification and confirmations
- War powers

Chapter 12: The Executive Branch and Its Relationship to Congress

- Presidential election and the Electoral College
- Executive orders and directives
- The federal bureaucracy
- Agency rulemaking and congressional review

Chapter 13: The Judicial Branch and Constitutional Interpretation

- Structure of the federal courts
- Supreme Court jurisdiction
- Judicial appointments and confirmation
- Marbury v. Madison and judicial review
- Originalism versus living constitutionalism
- Landmark constitutional cases

Chapter 14: Civil Liberties and Civil Rights

- Free speech and press protections
- Religious freedom and establishment
- Due process and equal protection
- Voting rights expansion

Chapter 15: Interest Groups, Parties, and Political Influence

- Political party development
- Lobbying and advocacy
- Campaign finance regulation
- Political action committees

Contents

Chapter 1: Origins of American Government

American governance didn't emerge from a vacuum in 1776. It grew from a century and a half of practical experience on North American soil, combined with centuries of English legal tradition and a sudden explosion of European intellectual curiosity. By the time the delegates met in Philadelphia, they weren't inventing a system, but were codifying a culture of self-rule that had already taken deep root in the colonies.

Colonial Governance and Self-Rule Traditions

English settlers brought their political habits with them, but the sheer distance from London necessitated immediate adaptation. In 1619, the Virginia Company established the **House of Burgesses**, the first elective governing body in British overseas possessions. This assembly allowed landowners to pass laws and levy taxes, creating a precedent for local control that later generations would defend as an inherent right. While the King technically held ultimate authority, the practical reality of a three thousand mile ocean meant that London's influence remained sporadic for much of the seventeenth century.

The Pilgrims added a different layer to this tradition with the **Mayflower Compact** in 1620. Because they landed outside their intended patent's jurisdiction, they faced a legal void. To prevent anarchy, the male passengers signed a covenant to form a "civil body politic" and obey the laws they collectively created. This document represents an early, practical application of the social contract. It wasn't a formal constitution, but it established the principle that government derives its legitimacy from the consent of the governed.

Colonial legislatures eventually became the dominant political force in every province. These bodies generally consisted of two houses: an upper house appointed by the governor or the King, and a lower house elected by property-holding men. The lower houses mirrored the British House of Commons, especially regarding the power of the purse. They controlled the governor's salary and the colonial budget. If a Royal Governor ignored the assembly's wishes, the assembly simply withheld his pay. This financial leverage gave colonists a sense of political agency that their counterparts in other empires lacked.

By the mid-eighteenth century, three types of colonies existed: royal, proprietary, and charter. In **royal colonies** like Virginia and New York, the King appointed the governor directly. **Proprietary colonies** like Pennsylvania and Maryland were essentially land grants to individuals or families who acted as mini-monarchs. **Charter colonies** like Connecticut and Rhode Island enjoyed the most independence, electing their own governors without royal interference. Despite these structural differences, a common thread of representative government ran through all of them.

(The Mayflower Compact functioned not just as a philosophical agreement but as an immediate risk-management agreement among investors and settlers. This way disputes over labor, land allocation, and survival resources could be adjudicated collectively rather than destabilizing the fragile colony.)

British policy for decades was characterized by **salutary neglect**. The Crown chose not to strictly enforce parliamentary laws, particularly trade regulations, as long as the colonies remained profitable and loyal. This period of unofficial autonomy allowed the colonies to develop their own legal codes, judicial systems, and tax structures. When Britain later tried to reassert direct control after 1763, the colonists didn't view it as a return to order; they saw it as an illegal seizure of the powers they had exercised for generations.

English Common Law Inheritance

The American legal system is a direct descendant of **English Common Law**, a body of unwritten law developed through judicial decisions rather than legislative statutes. This system relies on **precedent**, meaning judges look to past rulings to guide current cases. This approach ensures consistency and predictability, yet it also carries the weight of centuries of struggle between the English people and their monarchs.

The foundation of this tradition is the **Magna Carta** of 1215. King John signed this "Great Charter" under pressure from rebellious barons, agreeing that even the monarch was not above the law. It introduced the concept of **due process**, ensuring that no free man could be imprisoned or stripped of property except by the lawful judgment of his peers or the law of the land. Although it initially protected only the nobility, its principles eventually expanded to cover all subjects. American revolutionaries frequently cited the Magna Carta to argue that their rights were ancient and immutable.

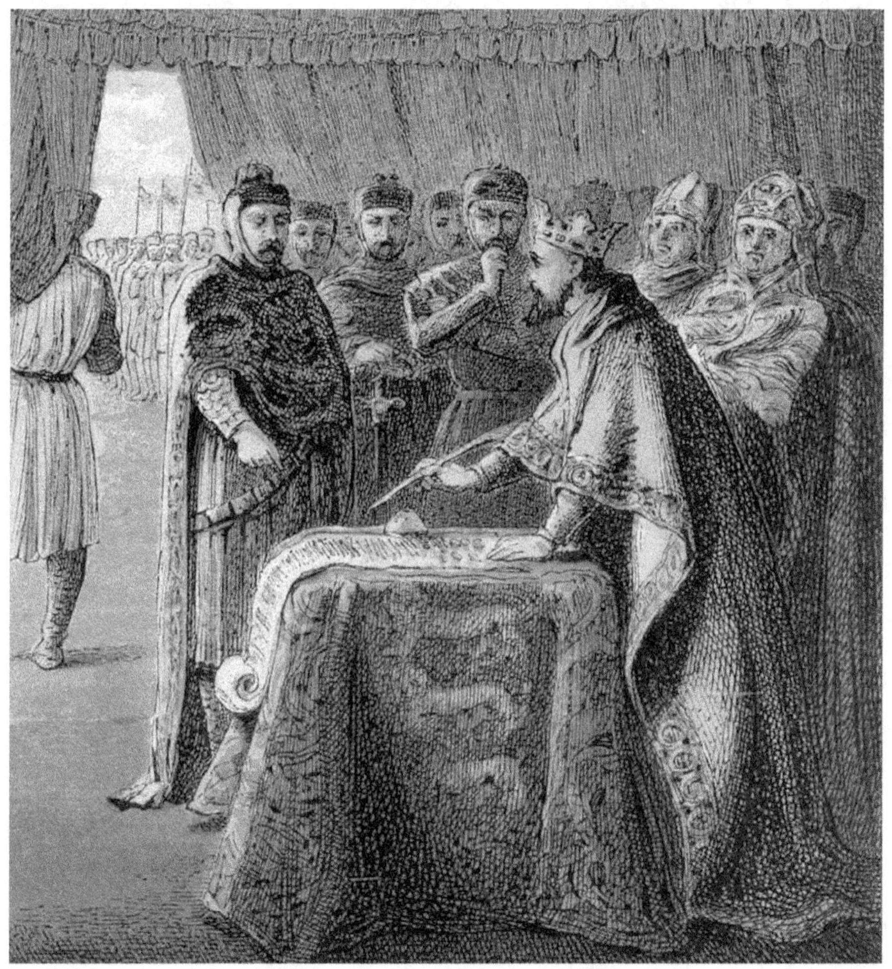

(The Magna Carta established that even the monarch was subject to law, introducing due process and limits on arbitrary authority. These principles were later embedded in American constitutionalism, especially in protections like habeas corpus, trial by jury, and constraints on executive power.)

In 1628, Parliament forced King Charles I to sign the **Petition of Right**. This document further limited royal power by prohibiting the king from levying taxes without parliamentary consent, housing soldiers in private homes, or imprisoning people without cause.

It reinforced the idea that the individual possessed specific protections that the state could not ignore. When the British government later violated these very principles in the 1760s, the colonists viewed the actions as a betrayal of the fundamental English constitution.

The **English Bill of Rights** of 1689 served as the final major piece of this legal inheritance. Following the Glorious Revolution, William and Mary accepted this document, which guaranteed frequent elections, freedom of speech within Parliament, and the right to petition the monarch. It also prohibited cruel and unusual punishments and excessive bail. You can see the DNA of the American Bill of Rights in these provisions. The American Founders didn't believe they were creating new rights; they believed they were claiming their birthright as "Englishmen."

Common law also established the **jury system**, which the colonists viewed as a vital defense against government overreach. In the famous 1735 trial of John Peter Zenger, a New York jury acquitted a printer of seditious libel because his criticisms of the governor were true. This case established that truth is a defense against libel charges and demonstrated how common law traditions could be used to protect emerging American values like freedom of the press.

Enlightenment Political Philosophy

While English law provided the skeletal structure of American government, the **Enlightenment** provided the intellectual muscle. This eighteenth-century movement emphasized reason, science, and individualism over tradition and religious dogma. The Founders were avid readers of European "philosophes," and they utilized these ideas to justify their break with Britain and the construction of a new Republic.

John Locke stands as the most influential figure for the American project. In his *Two Treatises of Government*, Locke challenged the "divine right of kings," arguing instead that all people are born with **natural rights** to life, liberty, and property. Locke posited that in a "state of nature" (a world without government) life would be chaotic because no one could reliably protect their rights. Therefore, people enter into a **social contract**, creating a government to protect those rights. If a government fails in this duty or becomes tyrannical, Locke argued, the people have a right and an obligation to overthrow it. Thomas Jefferson essentially summarized Locke's philosophy when he wrote the Declaration of Independence, merely swapping "property" for "the pursuit of happiness."

Baron de Montesquieu provided the structural solution to the problem of tyranny. In *The Spirit of the Laws*, he analyzed various forms of government and concluded that the best way to preserve liberty was through the **separation of powers**. He argued that the legislative, executive, and judicial functions should be held by different bodies to prevent any one person or group from gaining absolute control.

This idea became the blueprint for the American system of checks and balances. The Founders took Montesquieu's theories seriously, believing that human nature was inherently prone to corruption and that government must be designed to counteract that impulse.

Jean-Jacques Rousseau contributed the concept of **popular sovereignty**. In his version of the social contract, he argued that legitimate government must be based on the "general will" of the people. While Rousseau's ideas were sometimes more radical than those of the American Founders, his emphasis on the collective authority of the citizenry deeply influenced the Preamble of the Constitution. The phrase "We the People" is a direct nod to the idea that the government's power resides in the population, not in a monarch or a hereditary elite.

Thomas Hobbes offered a darker view of humanity that the Founders also considered. In *Leviathan*, he argued that human beings are naturally selfish and violent, and that without a strong, central authority, life would be "nasty, brutish, and short." While the Founders rejected Hobbes's call for an absolute dictator, they agreed with his assessment that a weak government leads to chaos. This tension, between the need for order (Hobbes) and the desire for liberty (Locke), defined the debates at the Constitutional Convention.

Voltaire (right) and his defense of civil liberties, particularly freedom of speech and religion, also left a mark. In an era when most European nations had state-sponsored churches that persecuted dissenters, the idea of religious pluralism was revolutionary. The American experiment with the separation of church and state was a direct application of Enlightenment skepticism toward institutionalized religious power.

Grievances Under British Rule

The transition from loyal subjects to revolutionaries was a slow, legalistic process. After the **French and Indian War** ended in 1763, Britain faced a massive national debt. Parliament believed the colonies should pay their share for the protection the British military provided. The colonists, however, viewed the new taxes and regulations as a violation of their established rights of self-government.

The **Proclamation of 1713** was the first major point of contention. It prohibited settlers from moving west of the Appalachian Mountains to avoid further conflict with Native Americans. For colonists who had fought the war specifically to gain access to that land, this was an intolerable restriction on their economic future. It signaled that the Crown's priorities were no longer aligned with the interests of the American people.

The **Stamp Act** of 1765 marked the first time Parliament levied a direct tax on the colonies, requiring a revenue stamp on all legal documents, newspapers, and even playing cards. Previous taxes were duties on trade, but the Stamp Act hit every aspect of daily colonial life. The response was the cry of **"No taxation without representation."** The colonists didn't necessarily object to the amount of the tax; they objected to the principle that a body three thousand miles away, in which they had no elected representatives, could take their money.

Britain responded with the **Declaratory Act**, which asserted Parliament's authority to bind the colonies "in all cases whatsoever." This was a direct rejection of the colonial assemblies' claim to exclusive taxing power. Tensions escalated with the **Townshend Acts**, which taxed imported goods like glass, lead, paint, and tea. To enforce these laws, Britain sent troops to Boston, leading to the **Boston Massacre** in 1770. While the event was largely accidental, colonial propagandists used it to paint the British military as a murderous force of occupation.

The **Tea Act** of 1773 was intended to save the struggling East India Company by allowing it to sell tea directly to the colonies at a discount, even with the tax. Colonists saw this as a bribe to accept parliamentary taxation and a move toward a monopoly.

The resulting **Boston Tea Party** prompted the harshest British response yet: the **Coercive Acts**, known in the colonies as the **Intolerable Acts**. These laws closed Boston Harbor, dissolved the Massachusetts legislature, and allowed British officials to be tried in England for crimes committed in the colonies.

(Often underemphasized, the Boston Tea Party was as much about constitutional principle as taxation. Colonists rejected Parliament's claim of virtual representation and the precedent of unchecked imperial authority. The destruction of East India Company tea also targeted monopoly power and corporate-state alignment. In the broader picture, it accelerated imperial retaliation and hardened colonial unity. It shifted resistance from protest to organized political revolution.)

These grievances transformed isolated colonial protests into a unified movement. The **First Continental Congress** met in 1774 to coordinate a resistance. They didn't initially seek independence; they wanted a return to the status quo of 1763. However, by the time the **Second Continental Congress** convened in 1775, blood had already been shed at Lexington and Concord. The King's refusal to answer the **Olive Branch Petition** and his declaration that the colonies were in "open and avowed rebellion" ended any hope of reconciliation.

The Declaration of Independence

In June 1776, Richard Henry Lee of Virginia introduced a resolution stating that "these United Colonies are, and of right ought to be, free and independent States."

The Congress appointed a committee of five to draft a formal statement explaining the decision to the world. While Benjamin Franklin and John Adams were on the committee, the primary authorship fell to **Thomas Jefferson**.

The Declaration of Independence is more than a breakup letter; it is a legal and philosophical brief. It is divided into four distinct parts: the Preamble, the Declaration of Natural Rights, the List of Grievances, and the Resolution of Independence. Jefferson's task was to prove that the King had broken the social contract, thereby justifying a revolution under Enlightenment principles.

Jefferson, though only 33, was chosen by the Committee of Five because of his exceptional writing ability and clear articulation of Enlightenment ideas, already demonstrated in works like *A Summary View of the Rights of British America*. John Adams, a leading advocate, deferred to him strategically, believing a Virginian author would unify colonies and carry broader legitimacy. Benjamin Franklin provided edits that refined tone and persuasion.

The Preamble and the section on natural rights contain the most famous language in American political history. Jefferson wrote:

> "We hold these truths to be self-evident, that all men are created equal, that they are endowed by their Creator with certain unalienable Rights, that among these are Life, Liberty and the pursuit of happiness."

This statement was revolutionary. It asserted that rights don't come from a king or a government, but from a higher source, making them "unalienable" – meaning they can't be taken away. Stating that "to secure these rights, Governments are instituted among Men, deriving their just powers from the consent of the governed," Jefferson firmly established the principle of **popular sovereignty**.

The bulk of the document is a long list of specific charges against **King George III**. By focusing the blame on the King rather than Parliament, the colonists were cutting their final tie to the British system. The grievances included:

- Taxing the colonies without their consent.
- Depriving them of the right to a trial by jury.
- Suspending their legislatures.
- Quartering large bodies of armed troops among them.
- Cutting off their trade with all parts of the world.

The Declaration concludes by stating that as "Free and Independent States," the new nation has the full power to levy war, conclude peace, contract alliances, and establish commerce. When the delegates signed the document, they were committing an act of high treason against the British Crown. They famously pledged to each other their "Lives, our Fortunes and our sacred Honor."

The Declaration didn't create a government. It was a statement of intent and a moral justification for war. It established the ideals toward which the new nation would strive, even if it didn't immediately live up to them. The contradiction between the claim that "all men are created equal" and the reality of chattel slavery would haunt American politics for nearly a century and lead to the nation's greatest crisis.

Articles of Confederation and Their Failures

After declaring independence, the Second Continental Congress needed to create a formal structure to manage the war effort and govern the thirteen states. The result was the **Articles of Confederation**, which was drafted in 1777 but not fully ratified until 1781. The Articles reflected the deep-seated fear of a strong central authority. Having just escaped the perceived tyranny of the British Crown, the Founders intentionally created a "league of friendship" rather than a unified nation.

Under the Articles, the states retained their **sovereignty**, freedom, and independence. The central government consisted of a single body, the **Confederation Congress**, where each state had exactly one vote, regardless of its population or size. There was no executive branch to enforce laws and no national judiciary to settle disputes between states. To pass any major legislation, nine of the thirteen states had to agree. To amend the Articles, the vote had to be unanimous. This structure made meaningful action nearly impossible.

The central government lacked the most basic power of a sovereign state: the **power to tax**. Congress could only "request" funds from the states. As you might expect, states rarely sent the full amount requested, leaving the national government perpetually broke and unable to pay its war debts. Furthermore, Congress had no power to regulate interstate or foreign commerce. Each state began issuing its own currency and placing tariffs on goods from neighboring states. New York taxed firewood from Connecticut and cabbages from New Jersey, creating economic friction that threatened to tear the confederation apart.

The weaknesses of the Articles were most evident in the realm of foreign policy and national security. The British refused to vacate their forts in the Northwest Territory, and the Spanish closed the Mississippi River to American trade. The central government was too weak to negotiate effectively or raise an army to defend its borders. When **Shays' Rebellion** broke out in Massachusetts in 1786, the federal government was powerless to help. Daniel Shays, a Revolutionary War veteran, led a group of debt-ridden farmers in an armed uprising to prevent foreclosures. The fact that a private militia had to be raised to put down the rebellion terrified the nation's leaders.

Feature	Articles of Confederation	U.S. Constitution (for comparison)
Executive	None	President
Legislature	Unicameral (One House)	Bicameral (House and Senate)
Taxation	States only	Both Federal and State
Commerce	State regulation	Federal regulation of interstate trade
Voting	One vote per state	Proportional (House) and Equal (Senate)
Amendments	Unanimous consent	Two-thirds of Congress + Three-fourths of States

Shays' Rebellion served as the catalyst for change. It proved that a government without the power to enforce its laws or protect property was a recipe for anarchy.

Nationalists like Alexander Hamilton and James Madison argued that the Articles were fundamentally flawed and could not be "fixed." They called for a meeting in Annapolis to discuss trade, which led to a broader call for a convention in Philadelphia to revise the Articles.

The Articles did have some successes, most notably the **Northwest Ordinance of 1787**. This law established a process for admitting new states to the Union on an equal footing with the original thirteen and prohibited slavery in the new territories. It provided a model for westward expansion that the nation would follow for decades. However, these successes couldn't outweigh the systemic failures of the central government.

The Articles of Confederation period was a "critical period" that taught the Founders what *not* to do. They learned that a government must have the authority to tax, the power to regulate trade, and an executive to carry out its will.

They realized that while liberty is essential, it must be balanced with order. By 1787, the consensus among the political elite was clear: the league of friendship had failed, and a more perfect union was required.

This realization set the stage for the Constitutional Convention. The delegates who traveled to Philadelphia weren't just thinking about the immediate crisis; they were looking back at the House of Burgesses, the Magna Carta, and the writings of Locke and Montesquieu. They were taking 150 years of colonial history and five years of confederation failure and attempting to forge a government that could survive the pressures of both human nature and international politics.

The struggle to define the American government was just beginning. While the Declaration established the *why* of the nation, and the Articles demonstrated the *how not* to govern, the delegates in Philadelphia were about to tackle the much more difficult task of determining the *how*. They had to create a system that was strong enough to protect the nation but limited enough to protect the individual. It was a balance that no nation in history had yet successfully struck.

The intellectual and political origins of the United States are a mix of inherited rights and radical new ideas. The colonists didn't invent the concept of liberty, but they did something unique: they took the theoretical ideals of the Enlightenment and turned them into a functioning, written system of law. They moved from the "rights of Englishmen" to the "rights of man," and finally to the "rights of American citizens." This transition was the essential prerequisite for the drafting of the Constitution. Without the lessons learned from colonial self-rule and the failures of the Articles, the American experiment likely would have ended before it truly began.

To what extent did the transition from the "rights of Englishmen" to the "rights of man" fundamentally change the legal arguments used to justify the American Revolution?

Chapter 2: The Constitutional Convention

In May 1787, fifty-five men gathered in Philadelphia with a mandate to revise the Articles of Confederation. The weather was unseasonably hot, the windows of the Pennsylvania State House were nailed shut to ensure secrecy, and the atmosphere inside was thick with tension. Most delegates realized within days that the Articles were beyond repair. They weren't there to patch a sinking ship; they were there to build a new vessel entirely. What followed was a summer of grueling debate, fragile alliances, and the most significant political engineering in human history.

Delegates and Their Competing Interests

The men who assembled in Philadelphia were not a representative cross-section of the American population. They were lawyers, merchants, planters, and revolutionary veterans. Most were wealthy, all were male, and all were white. Despite these demographic similarities, they were far from a monolith. Their interests were divided by geography, economy, and differing philosophies on the nature of power.

James Madison arrived as the most prepared man in the room. He had spent months studying historical confederacies and republics, concluding that a weak central government was a recipe for national suicide. He acted as the convention's primary architect and unofficial record-keeper. Beside him stood **Alexander Hamilton**, a staunch nationalist who believed the British system was the best in the world and wanted an executive with near-monarchal powers. Both men represented the "large state" or "nationalist" faction, which sought to shift authority away from state capitals and toward a central capital.

Benjamin Franklin, the oldest delegate at eighty-one, provided a calming presence during the most heated moments. George Washington, who presided over the convention, said little during the debates but gave the proceedings immediate legitimacy. His presence signaled that this wasn't a radical coup but a necessary evolution of the Revolution. Without Washington's participation, it's unlikely the public would have ever accepted the resulting document.

Conflict arose quickly between the "large states" like Virginia, Pennsylvania, and Massachusetts, and "small states" like New Jersey, Delaware, and Maryland. The large states wanted representation based on population; they believed it was only fair that more people should have more influence. The small states feared they would be swallowed by their larger neighbors. They viewed their state sovereignty as a shield and insisted on equal representation, regardless of population size.

Economic interests also clashed. Northern delegates, representing emerging commercial hubs, wanted the national government to have the power to regulate trade and set tariffs. Southern delegates, whose wealth depended on an agricultural export economy fueled by enslaved labor, feared that a Northern-dominated Congress would use trade powers to tax their exports or, worse, abolish the slave trade. These weren't just abstract philosophical disagreements; they were existential threats to the delegates' way of life.

The decision to work in absolute secrecy was the first major tactical move. The delegates agreed that no one should speak of the proceedings outside the hall, and no notes should be published. This allowed men to change their minds without fear of public backlash and encouraged honest, sometimes brutal, debate. It also prevented outside interest groups from lobbying the delegates or whipping up public hysteria before the plan was finished.

The Virginia Plan

James Madison didn't wait for the convention to begin before setting the agenda. He arrived in Philadelphia with a comprehensive proposal known as the **Virginia Plan**, which Edmund Randolph introduced on the fourth day of the convention. This plan didn't just suggest tweaks to the Articles; it proposed a radical restructuring of the entire American political system.

The Virginia Plan called for a strong **national government** with three distinct branches: legislative, executive, and judicial. This was a direct application of Montesquieu's theory of separated powers. The most controversial feature was the proposed bicameral legislature, where representation in both houses would be based on either a state's population or the amount of money it contributed to the federal treasury. This gave a massive advantage to the most populous states.

Under this plan, the lower house would be elected directly by the people. This house would then elect the members of the upper house from a list of candidates nominated by state legislatures.

Together, these two houses would choose the national executive and the national judiciary. This meant the legislature would be the supreme power in the government, effectively holding the keys to the other two branches.

The Virginia Plan gave Congress the power to legislate in all cases where the states were "incompetent" or where state laws might disrupt national harmony. Perhaps most radically, it proposed a "Council of Revision" consisting of the executive and members of the judiciary. This council would have the authority to veto acts passed by the national legislature. Even more startling to the small-state delegates was the provision giving the national legislature the power to negate any state law it deemed inconsistent with the articles of union.

Madison was essentially arguing that the states had failed. He believed that the only way to prevent the "tyranny of the majority" within individual states, specifically regarding property rights and debt relief, was to create an overarching national authority. The Virginia Plan shifted the locus of sovereignty from the states to the people. It treated the United States as a single nation rather than a collection of independent entities.

(The most enduring legacy of the Virginia Plan wasn't just its structure; it was that it established **population as the default logic of political power at the national level**, even though it initially failed in pure form. While the Great Compromise modified it, the House of Representatives still reflects Madison's core principle that legitimacy flows from the people in proportion to their numbers, not from states as equal units. This quietly redefined sovereignty: over time, national politics would be driven more by demographic weight than by state equality, shaping everything from elections to policy priorities.)

Small-state delegates were horrified. They saw this as a move toward a consolidated government that would render their local governments irrelevant. They argued that the convention had no legal authority to create such a system. They reminded the room that the states had sent them there to "revise" the Articles, not to destroy them. The debate over the Virginia Plan lasted for two weeks, pushing the convention to its first major breaking point.

The New Jersey Plan

On June 15, William Paterson of New Jersey introduced a counter-proposal. The **New Jersey Plan** was a direct response to the "nationalist" vision of Madison and Hamilton. It was designed to protect the interests of the smaller states by retaining the core structure of the Articles of Confederation while adding just enough power to keep the government from collapsing.

The New Jersey Plan proposed a **unicameral legislature** where each state would continue to have exactly one vote. This maintained the principle of state equality that had existed since the First Continental Congress. It rejected the idea of proportional representation entirely, arguing that a confederation is a compact between equal sovereigns, not a union of individuals. Paterson famously asked why a large state should have more power simply because it had more people, comparing the states to individuals in a state of nature.

While it kept the single-house legislature, the plan did grant Congress two powers it desperately lacked: the authority to levy taxes and the power to regulate interstate and foreign commerce. It also created a multi-person executive branch, elected by Congress, which would be removable by a majority of state governors. This was a deliberate attempt to prevent the rise of a single, powerful leader who might resemble a monarch.

Crucially, the New Jersey Plan introduced a version of what would later become the **Supremacy Clause**. It stated that acts of Congress and treaties would be the "supreme law of the respective States."

This was a significant concession; it admitted that federal law must override state law in specific areas to prevent the chaos of the previous decade. However, it didn't give Congress the power to veto state laws generally, as the Virginia Plan had proposed.

The New Jersey Plan was essentially a "federal" plan rather than a "national" one. It envisioned the central government as an agent of the states, performing specific, limited tasks that the states couldn't handle on their own. It appealed to those who feared that a distant national government would be just as oppressive as the British Parliament had been. For many delegates, the New Jersey Plan represented the safe, moderate path.

However, the nationalists weren't interested in moderate fixes. Madison and Hamilton argued that the New Jersey Plan didn't go far enough to solve the systemic problems of the country. They pointed out that a government that couldn't act directly on individuals, but had to rely on state cooperation, was doomed to fail. After intense debate, the convention voted to reject the New Jersey Plan and proceed with the Virginia Plan as the working blueprint. This decision nearly ended the convention, as the small states threatened to leave.

The Great Compromise

By July, the convention had reached a stalemate. The issue of representation was the "Gordian Knot" that no one seemed able to cut. The large states refused to give up proportional representation, and the small states refused to accept it. Roger Sherman of Connecticut, a man known for his pragmatic approach to politics, eventually offered the solution that saved the convention: the **Great Compromise**, also known as the Connecticut Compromise.

Sherman proposed a bicameral legislature that split the difference between the two plans. In the lower house, the **House of Representatives**, representation would be based on population. This satisfied the large states and the principle of popular sovereignty. In the upper house, the **Senate**, each state would have equal representation, exactly two senators, regardless of size. This satisfied the small states and the principle of state sovereignty.

To sweeten the deal for the large states, Sherman included a provision that all bills for raising or spending money must originate in the House of Representatives. Since the House was the body where the larger populations had more influence, this gave the more populous states a degree of control over the national purse. This was a critical detail; it meant that the people, through their more direct representatives, would have the first say in how their tax dollars were collected and spent.

The debate over this compromise was brutal. Madison initially hated it. He believed that equal representation in the Senate was a violation of justice and that it would allow a minority of the population to block the will of the majority. He argued that it was a step back toward the failures of the Articles. On the other side, delegates from Delaware and New Jersey hinted that they might seek foreign alliances if they weren't given equal standing in the new government.

A special committee was formed to hammer out the details. Eventually, the pragmatists won out over the ideologues. On July 16, the convention narrowly passed the Great Compromise.

This decision fundamentally changed the nature of the American republic. It created a "partly national, partly federal" system. The House represented the American people as a single nation, while the Senate represented the states as political entities.

This structure created an inherent tension that remains in American politics today. It ensures that no legislation can pass without the support of both a majority of the people (via the House) and a majority of the states (via the Senate). It protects the minority interests of smaller states from being steamrolled by the massive populations of urban centers. While it may lead to legislative gridlock, the Founders viewed this as a feature, not a bug. They wanted a system where change was difficult and required broad consensus.

The Three-Fifths Compromise

Once the delegates agreed that the House of Representatives would be based on population, a new and more toxic question emerged: who should be counted? The divide shifted from large versus small states to North versus South.

Specifically, the convention had to decide whether enslaved people should be included in the population totals used to determine a state's number of representatives.

Southern delegates, particularly those from South Carolina and Georgia, insisted that enslaved people be counted fully. This was a purely political play for power. Southern states wanted more seats in the House and more votes in the Electoral College, but they had no intention of granting enslaved people any rights or recognizing their humanity. Northern delegates pointed out the blatant hypocrisy of this position. If enslaved people were legally considered property, why should they be counted as people for representation?

The debate was one of the few times the morality of slavery was explicitly addressed on the convention floor. Gouverneur Morris of Pennsylvania delivered a blistering speech, calling slavery a "nefarious institution" and the "curse of heaven."

He argued that counting enslaved people would essentially reward the Southern states for their involvement in the slave trade. He suggested that if the South wanted them counted, they should make them citizens.

The South responded with an ultimatum. Pierce Butler and Charles Pinckney of South Carolina made it clear that their states would not join the Union if their "property" wasn't accounted for in the political balance. The Northern states, fearing that the convention would collapse and the states would descend into civil war or foreign conquest, opted for a cold, political calculation.

The result was the **Three-Fifths Compromise**. It stated that for purposes of representation and direct taxation, a state's population would be determined by counting the "whole number of free persons" and "three-fifths of all other persons." The term "slave" was never used in the Constitution; the Founders used euphemisms to avoid staining the document with the explicit word, even as they codified the institution's political influence.

Aspect	Northern View	Southern View	Compromise Result
Status of Enslaved People	Property; no political weight	People for representation only	Three-fifths of a person for count
Taxation	Should be taxed as property	Should not be taxed	Counted for both taxes and seats
Political Goal	Limit Southern power	Maximize Southern power	Southern dominance in the House

This compromise gave the South a significant boost in political power for the next seventy years. It meant that Southern white voters had more influence per capita than Northern voters. This "slave power" would eventually allow the South to control the Presidency, the Speakership of the House, and the Supreme Court for much of the antebellum period. While the compromise kept the South in the convention, it baked an inherent injustice into the foundation of the government that would eventually require a civil war to resolve.

Commerce, the Slave Trade, and the Executive

As the convention moved into its final weeks, the delegates had to settle the remaining details of the executive branch and national commerce. These issues were often linked in backroom deals. Northern states wanted the federal government to have the power to regulate commerce with a simple majority vote. Southern states, fearing Northern control over their trade, demanded a two-thirds supermajority for any navigation acts.

The "Commerce and Slave Trade Compromise" resolved this. The South agreed to allow Congress to regulate commerce with a simple majority. In exchange, the North agreed to a provision that forbade Congress from banning the **Atlantic Slave Trade** for twenty years (until 1808).

Additionally, a **Fugitive Slave Clause** was added, requiring Northern states to return enslaved people who had escaped their masters. This was the second major concession to the South, and it further embedded slavery into the legal fabric of the nation.

The design of the executive branch also sparked intense debate. Some delegates wanted a committee to lead the country, fearing that a single president would become a tyrant. Others, like Hamilton, wanted a single executive with a life term. The convention eventually settled on a single **President** with a four-year term, but they couldn't agree on how to elect this person.

The options were direct election by the people, election by Congress, or election by state legislatures. Direct election was rejected because many delegates didn't trust the general public to have enough information to make a wise choice. Election by Congress was rejected because it would make the President a puppet of the legislature, violating the separation of powers. The solution was the **Electoral College**.

This system allowed each state to appoint "electors" equal to its total number of representatives and senators. These electors would then cast votes for the President. It was a convoluted system designed to be a buffer between the "mob" and the executive office, while still giving the states a role in the process. It was another example of the "partly national, partly federal" character of the new government. It satisfied the small states because it guaranteed them a minimum of three electoral votes, regardless of how small their population was.

By September, the document was mostly complete. The delegates had created a system of **enumerated powers**, listing specifically what the federal government could do and leaving the rest to the states or the people. They included a "Necessary and Proper Clause" to allow for future flexibility, and a judicial branch that would eventually claim the power to interpret the document itself.

On September 17, 1787, thirty-nine of the remaining delegates signed the Constitution. Some, like George Mason and Elbridge Gerry, refused to sign because the document lacked a Bill of Rights. As the delegates left the hall, a woman famously asked Benjamin Franklin what kind of government they had created. He replied, "A republic, if you can keep it."

The Constitutional Convention succeeded where the Articles of Confederation had failed because the delegates were willing to prioritize the survival of the union over their own specific interests. They didn't create a perfect document; they created a functional one. They left many questions unanswered, most notably the ultimate fate of slavery and the exact line between state and federal power, but they provided a framework that was strong enough to hold the states together and flexible enough to grow. The "miracle at Philadelphia" wasn't that they agreed on everything, but that they agreed to stay in the room until they found a way to live together.

The work, however, was only half done. The document now had to be sent to the states for ratification. The debates in Philadelphia had been private, but the debates in the state conventions would be very public and much more volatile. The Federalist and Anti-Federalist papers were about to begin, and the future of the American experiment still hung in the balance.

The convention proved that the American people were capable of "establishing good government from reflection and choice," rather than being forever destined to depend on "accident and force," as Alexander Hamilton later wrote. It was a triumph of deliberate political design. The compromises made in that hot Philadelphia room (the Great Compromise, the Three-Fifths Compromise, and the creation of the Electoral College) defined the shape of American democracy for centuries. Whether those compromises were a stroke of genius or a deal with the devil remains a central question of American history.

Was the Great Compromise a necessary practical solution for national survival, or did it create a permanent structural defect by giving disproportionate power to smaller states?

Chapter 3: Structure and Text of the Constitution

The United States Constitution is a surprisingly brief document, consisting of roughly 4,500 words in its original form. It isn't a dense legal code or a comprehensive list of every possible law.

Instead, it serves as a skeletal framework that defines the boundaries of federal authority. Drafting a written constitution, the Founders rejected the British model of an "unwritten" constitution based on custom and scattered statutes. They wanted a clear, accessible set of rules that both the governors and the governed could reference.

The Preamble and Its Purpose

The Preamble is the Constitution's mission statement. While it carries no direct legal weight in court, meaning a lawyer cannot sue the government based solely on a violation of the Preamble, it establishes the document's intent and source of authority.

The opening phrase, **"We the People,"** represents a seismic shift in political thought. It signaled that the government's legitimacy didn't flow from the states as independent entities, nor from a divine monarch, but from the collective citizenry. This is the clearest expression of **popular sovereignty** in the entire document. It defines the United States as a single political community rather than a mere league of sovereign states.

The Preamble then outlines six specific goals for the new government:

1. **To form a more perfect Union -** This was a direct acknowledgment that the Articles of Confederation had failed to keep the states cohesive.
2. **Establish Justice -** The Founders wanted a national system of courts to replace the inconsistent and often biased state-level legal proceedings.
3. **Insure domestic Tranquility -** This goal was a response to internal unrest like Shays' Rebellion. The government needed the power to maintain order within its borders.
4. **Provide for the common defense -** The nation required a unified military capability to protect against foreign powers like Britain and Spain.
5. **Promote the general Welfare -** This broad phrase allowed the government to look after the economic and social well-being of the nation as a whole.
6. **Secure the Blessings of Liberty -** The document was intended to protect the freedom won in the Revolution for both the current generation and "posterity."

These objectives provide a yardstick for measuring the government's performance. They also establish that the Constitution is a forward-looking document. By stating the purpose was to secure liberty for "posterity," the Framers indicated they were building a system intended to endure for centuries, not just to solve the immediate crises of the 1780s.

Article-by-Article Overview

The main body of the Constitution is divided into seven Articles. Each Article addresses a different component of the federal structure or the relationship between the states and the national government. The order of these articles isn't accidental; it reflects the Founders' priorities.

Article I is the longest and most detailed section of the Constitution, focusing on the **Legislative Branch**. The Framers believed that in a representative republic, the legislature should be the most significant branch because it is closest to the people. It establishes the **bicameral** structure consisting of the House of Representatives and the Senate. It details the qualifications for office, the methods of election, and the specific procedures for making laws. Most importantly, Section 8 of Article I lists the specific powers granted to Congress, providing the legal basis for most federal activity.

Article II establishes the **Executive Branch**. It is significantly shorter and less specific than Article I, which has led to centuries of debate over the exact limits of presidential power. It describes the office of the President and Vice President, the four-year term, and the Electoral College. It also outlines the President's responsibilities as Commander in Chief, the power to make treaties (with Senate approval), and the duty to "take Care that the Laws be faithfully executed." This "Take Care" clause is the foundation of the President's administrative authority over the federal bureaucracy.

Article III creates the **Judicial Branch**. Interestingly, it only specifically identifies one court: the **Supreme Court**. It leaves the creation of "inferior" or lower federal courts to Congress. This article defines the types of cases federal courts can hear (jurisdiction) and guarantees a trial by jury in criminal cases. It also provides a very narrow definition of treason to prevent the government from using the charge as a political weapon against dissenters. A key feature of Article III is that federal judges hold their offices during "good Behavior," which effectively means life tenure, insulating them from political pressure.

Article IV governs **Relations Among the States**. This section was vital for turning thirteen separate entities into a single nation. The **Full Faith and Credit Clause** requires states to respect the public acts, records, and judicial proceedings of every other state. For example, a contract signed in Pennsylvania remains valid if the parties move to Georgia. The **Privileges and Immunities Clause** prevents states from discriminating against citizens of other states. It also outlines the process for admitting new states and guarantees that every state will have a "Republican Form of Government." This framework also enables interstate mobility and commerce by reducing legal fragmentation that would otherwise deter contracts, travel, and business across state lines. At the same time, the "Republican Form of Government" guarantee gives the federal government a constitutional basis to intervene if a state's political system departs from representative rule.

Article V describes the **Amendment Process**. The Framers knew the document wasn't perfect and would need to change as the nation grew. However, they wanted the process to be difficult enough to prevent "factions" from making impulsive changes. There are two ways to propose an amendment: a two-thirds vote in both houses of Congress or a national convention called by two-thirds of the states. To be ratified, an amendment must be approved by three-fourths of the state legislatures or three-fourths of state conventions. This high bar ensures that any change to the supreme law of the land has broad, national support.

Article VI contains the **Supremacy Clause**. It states that the Constitution, federal laws, and treaties are the "supreme Law of the Land." This means that if a state law conflicts with a valid federal law, the federal law prevails. This article also requires all federal and state officials to take an oath to support the Constitution and explicitly prohibits any "religious Test" as a qualification for holding public office. This was a radical departure from many state constitutions of the time, which often required officeholders to be of a specific faith.

Article VII details the **Ratification** process. It stated that the Constitution would take effect once nine of the thirteen states approved it in special ratifying conventions. This was a clever move by the Federalists. From bypassing the state legislatures, which stood to lose power under the new system, and going directly to conventions elected by the people, the Framers gave the Constitution a more direct claim to popular legitimacy.

Enumerated Powers

The United States government is a government of **delegated powers**. This means it only possesses the authority specifically granted to it by the Constitution. Any power not given to the federal government remains with the states or the people. This principle of **limited government** is central to the American political identity.

The **Enumerated Powers** (also called Expressed Powers) are those specifically listed in the text, primarily in Article I, Section 8. These include:

- The power to lay and collect taxes.
- The power to borrow money on the credit of the United States.
- The power to regulate commerce with foreign nations and among the states (the **Commerce Clause**).
- The power to coin money and regulate its value.
- The power to establish post offices and post roads.
- The power to declare war.
- The power to raise and support armies and a navy.

These powers were chosen to address the specific failures of the Articles of Confederation. Giving the federal government the authority to tax and regulate trade, the Framers ensured the nation would have a stable economy. By giving it the power to declare war and maintain a military, they ensured national security.

The list of enumerated powers acts as a boundary. When the federal government acts, it must be able to point to a specific clause in the Constitution that justifies its action. If it cannot, that action is technically unconstitutional. This creates a "checked" system where the government must constantly justify its reach.

Implied Powers

If the Constitution only allowed the government to do what was explicitly written in the text, the system would have become obsolete within a few decades. The world changes faster than parchment can be updated. To account for this, the Framers included the **Necessary and Proper Clause** at the end of Article I, Section 8.

This clause grants Congress the power to "make all Laws which shall be necessary and proper for carrying into Execution the foregoing Powers." These are known as **Implied Powers**. They aren't written out in detail, but they are logically derived from the enumerated powers. This clause is often called the **"Elastic Clause"** because it allows the reach of Congress to expand or contract based on the needs of the time.

The landmark Supreme Court case ***McCulloch v. Maryland*** (1819) solidified the doctrine of implied powers. The case centered on whether Congress had the authority to create a national bank, something not mentioned in the Constitution. Chief Justice John Marshall ruled that while the word "bank" isn't in Article I, the power to create one is implied by the enumerated powers to tax, borrow money, and regulate commerce. Marshall famously wrote, "Let the end be legitimate, let it be within the scope of the constitution, and all means which are appropriate... are constitutional."

Implied powers allow the government to address modern issues that the Founders could never have imagined. For example:

- The power to regulate interstate commerce implies the power to regulate television, radio, and the internet.
- The power to raise an army implies the power to enact a military draft.
- The power to collect taxes implies the power to create the Internal Revenue Service (IRS).

The relationship between enumerated and implied powers creates a constant tug-of-war in American law. Strict constructionists argue that implied powers should be interpreted narrowly to prevent the federal government from becoming too powerful. Loose constructionists (or broad constructionists) argue that the Elastic Clause should be interpreted generously to allow the government to solve complex national problems.

The Separation of Powers in the Text

The structure of the first three articles provides the mechanical basis for the **separation of powers**. By placing the legislative, executive, and judicial powers in separate articles, the Framers created a functional wall between them. This wasn't just for efficiency; it was a safeguard against tyranny.

In the original text, this separation is reinforced by different methods of selection and different term lengths. The House of Representatives was the only part of the federal government directly elected by the people (originally). Senators were chosen by state legislatures (until the 17th Amendment). The President was chosen by the Electoral College. Judges were appointed by the President and confirmed by the Senate.

This staggered system ensures that no single "wave" of popular opinion can take control of the entire government at once. Even if a radical movement swept the House elections, the Senate and the Presidency would remain as buffers. The diverse sources of authority mean that each branch answers to a different constituency, forcing them to compete and cooperate rather than conspire.

The Role of the Supremacy Clause

Article VI, Clause 2, the Supremacy Clause, is the "linchpin" of the entire federal system. Without it, the Constitution would be a set of suggestions that states could ignore at will. It establishes a clear hierarchy of law in the United States.

At the top is the Constitution itself. Below that are federal laws and treaties. At the bottom are state constitutions and state laws. If a state passes a law that contradicts a federal statute, provided the federal statute is constitutional, the state law is void. This ensures that the United States functions as a single legal entity rather than fifty separate ones.

The Supremacy Clause does not mean the federal government can do whatever it wants. It only applies when the federal government is acting within its constitutional authority (either enumerated or implied).

If Congress passes a law in an area where it has no delegated power, such as local education or general police powers, that law is not supreme because it is unconstitutional. The Supreme Court serves as the ultimate arbiter in these disputes, determining where state authority ends and federal authority begins.

This hierarchy is essential for a functioning national economy. Imagine if every state had different rules for what could be shipped across its borders or different standards for legal contracts. The Supremacy Clause, combined with the Commerce Clause, prevents this fragmented reality. It creates a "level playing field" for commerce and ensures that fundamental rights are protected consistently across state lines.

Checks and Balances within the Articles

While the separation of powers divides the government into three branches, the system of **checks and balances** allows each branch to monitor and limit the others. The text of the first three articles is peppered with these mechanisms.

For example, Article I gives Congress the power to pass laws, but Article II gives the President the power to veto them. To prevent the President from being a dictator, Article I allows Congress to override that veto with a two-thirds vote. Article II allows the President to make treaties and appoint judges, but Article I requires the "Advice and Consent" of the Senate for those actions to take effect.

Article III gives the courts the power to hear cases, but Article I gives Congress the power to determine the size of the Supreme Court and create lower courts. The most significant check is the power of **impeachment**, detailed in Articles I and II. The House has the power to charge (impeach) a President or federal judge with "Treason, Bribery, or other high Crimes and Misdemeanors," while the Senate holds the trial to determine if they should be removed from office.

These checks ensure that power is never absolute. Each branch is dependent on the others to function. The President needs Congress for money; Congress needs the President to sign bills; both need the Courts to interpret and enforce the law.

This interdependence forces compromise and prevents any single branch from dominating the others. It creates a system of "ambition countering ambition," as James Madison famously wrote.

A Living Blueprint

The structure of the Constitution is a masterpiece of political compromise and foresight. It provides enough detail to create a stable government but enough ambiguity to allow for growth. The distinction between enumerated and implied powers gives the government the strength to act when necessary while keeping it tethered to the original grant of authority.

The document's brevity is its greatest strength. By not trying to answer every question, the Framers left room for future generations to interpret the text in light of new challenges. The Preamble sets the high-minded goals, the Articles provide the functional machinery, and the Supremacy Clause ensures the whole system holds together.

Understanding the text of the Constitution requires looking past the individual clauses and seeing the system as a whole. It is a machine with many moving parts, all designed to balance the competing needs of liberty and order. As we move into the specifics of how this government was ratified and how the Bill of Rights was added, the importance of this structural foundation becomes even clearer. The Constitution is the "grand design" that transformed a collection of struggling colonies into a continental power.

Does the existence of "implied powers" through the Necessary and Proper Clause effectively render the concept of "enumerated powers" obsolete in a modern, complex society?

Chapter 4: Ratification and the Bill of Rights

The signing of the Constitution on September 17, 1787, did not create a new government. It merely proposed one. The document was a draft submitted to the American people for their approval or rejection. According to Article VII, the new system would only go into effect once nine of the thirteen states ratified it through special conventions. This process sparked the first great national political debate in American history, dividing the country into two camps: the **Federalists**, who supported the Constitution, and the **Anti-Federalists**, who feared it.

This struggle wasn't merely over administrative details; it was a fundamental argument about the nature of power, the necessity of centralized authority, and the protection of individual liberty. The outcome was never certain. In several key states, the vote was razor-thin. The debate forced the proponents of the Constitution to articulate a sophisticated political theory that remains the foundation of American governance today. It also led directly to the creation of the Bill of Rights, a set of protections that many Founders initially thought were unnecessary but which the people demanded as a condition for their consent.

Anti-Federalist Objections

The Anti-Federalists were not a single, unified political party but a loose collection of activists, writers, and politicians who shared a deep skepticism of the Philadelphia plan. Their ranks included prominent figures like Patrick Henry, George Mason, and Richard Henry Lee. While their specific concerns varied, they shared a central thesis: the proposed Constitution created a "consolidated" government that would eventually destroy the sovereignty of the states and the liberties of the individual.

Many Anti-Federalists wrote under pseudonyms like "Brutus," "Centinel," and "The Federal Farmer." Brutus, widely believed to be New York judge Robert Yates, penned a series of essays that targeted the **Necessary and Proper Clause** and the **Supremacy Clause**. He argued that these provisions gave the federal government a "blank check" to expand its power indefinitely. If federal law is always supreme, Brutus reasoned, then state constitutions and state laws would eventually be reduced to irrelevance. He predicted that the federal government would use its taxing power to drain the states of resources, leaving them as mere administrative shells.

The lack of a **Bill of Rights** was the most effective and popular Anti-Federalist argument. They pointed out that the Constitution listed the powers of the government but failed to list the rights of the people. To the Anti-Federalists, this was a dangerous omission. If the government had the power to raise an army, what prevented it from using that army to suppress free speech? If it could regulate commerce, what stopped it from banning certain books? They rejected the Federalist claim that a list of rights was unnecessary because the government only had delegated powers. They argued that history proved rulers would always seek to expand their authority unless specifically restrained by written barriers.

Anti-Federalists also attacked the scale of the proposed republic. Drawing on the ideas of Montesquieu, they argued that a free republic could only exist in a small territory where the citizens shared similar interests and could personally know their representatives. In a vast, continental empire, they claimed, the representatives would be distant from the people and easily corrupted by the luxuries of the capital. They feared the Senate would become an aristocratic "house of lords" and the President would evolve into an elective monarch.

Their concerns were rooted in the recent memory of the Revolution. They viewed the Constitution as a betrayal of the principles of 1776. To many Anti-Federalists, the Philadelphia convention had exceeded its mandate by scrapping the Articles of Confederation entirely. They saw the new system as a "top-down" imposition by a wealthy elite who wanted to protect their investments and suppress the populist impulses of the state legislatures.

Federalist Arguments

The Federalists, led by Alexander Hamilton, James Madison, and John Jay, countered these fears with a new "science of politics." Their most famous defense appeared in **The Federalist Papers**, a series of 85 essays published in New York newspapers under the name "Publius." These essays were designed to persuade New York voters to ratify the Constitution, but they quickly became the definitive interpretation of the document's intent.

James Madison provided the intellectual core of the Federalist argument. In **Federalist No. 10**, he addressed the Anti-Federalist claim that a large republic could not survive. Madison turned this argument on its head. He argued that "factions" (groups of citizens with interests contrary to the rights of others or the interests of the community) were the greatest threat to a republic.

In a small republic, a single faction could easily gain a majority and oppress the minority. In a large, "extended" republic, however, there would be so many different factions and interests that it would be nearly impossible for a permanent majority to form. The very size of the country would act as a check on tyranny.

In **Federalist No. 51**, Madison explained the mechanical safeguards within the Constitution. He famously wrote:

> "Ambition must be made to counteract ambition. The interest of the man must be connected with the constitutional rights of the place."

The Federalists argued that the **separation of powers** and the system of **checks and balances** made a Bill of Rights unnecessary. Because the government was divided into three competing branches, no single entity could ever accumulate enough power to become tyrannical. They viewed the Constitution itself as a Bill of Rights because it limited the government to a specific list of functions.

Alexander Hamilton added a pragmatic layer to the debate. In several essays, he emphasized the weakness of the Articles of Confederation and the danger of foreign intervention. He argued that without a strong central government, the states would fall into civil war or become pawns of European powers like Britain and France. Hamilton stressed the need for "energy in the executive," arguing that a vigorous president was essential for national security and the steady administration of laws.

Federalists also addressed the specific charge regarding the lack of a Bill of Rights. Hamilton argued in **Federalist No. 84** that such a list would actually be dangerous. If you list specific rights that the government can't violate, he reasoned, it implies that the government has the power to violate any right *not* on that list.

Why declare that things shall not be done which there is no power to do? The Federalists eventually realized, however, that this logical argument was losing the political battle. To win over the "middle-ground" delegates in the state conventions, they were forced to promise that a Bill of Rights would be the first order of business for the new Congress.

State Ratifying Conventions

The ratification process was a state-by-state struggle. The Federalists had several advantages: they were better organized, they controlled most of the newspapers, and they had the immense prestige of George Washington and Benjamin Franklin on their side. The smaller states, realizing they stood to gain protection and economic stability, ratified quickly. Delaware, Pennsylvania, New Jersey, Georgia, and Connecticut joined the new union within months of the convention's end.

The real battle took place in the large, influential states of **Massachusetts**, **Virginia**, and **New York**. In Massachusetts, the convention was initially dominated by Anti-Federalists. The tide turned only when Federalists proposed the "Massachusetts Compromise." They suggested that the state ratify the Constitution immediately but include a list of recommended amendments. This allowed hesitant delegates to support the new government while still signaling their demand for protections of individual rights. This strategy became the model for the remaining states.

The debate in Virginia was a clash of titans. Patrick Henry, the great orator of the Revolution, led the opposition, painting a terrifying picture of a federal "monster" that would tax the people into poverty.

James Madison, though not a powerful speaker, countered with calm, logical explanations of the Constitution's limits. The influence of George Washington, who didn't attend the convention but whose support was well-known, proved decisive. Virginia ratified by a narrow vote of 89 to 79.

In New York, the Anti-Federalists held a two-to-one majority when the convention began. Alexander Hamilton led a relentless pro-ratification campaign, using the Federalist Papers and the news of Virginia's ratification as leverage. He warned that if New York did not join, the city of New York might secede from the state to join the Union on its own. New York finally ratified by a vote of 30 to 27.

State	Date of Ratification	Vote Count
Delaware	December 7, 1787	30-0
Pennsylvania	December 12, 1787	46-23
Massachusetts	February 6, 1788	187-168
Virginia	June 25, 1788	89-79
New York	July 26, 1788	30-27
Rhode Island	May 29, 1790	34-32

North Carolina and Rhode Island were the final holdouts. North Carolina refused to ratify until a Bill of Rights was actually submitted to the states. Rhode Island, which had not even sent delegates to the Philadelphia convention, only joined after the new government threatened to treat it as a foreign nation and cut off trade. By 1790, the thirteen states were finally united under the new framework.

The First Ten Amendments (The Bill of Rights)

True to their word, the Federalists moved quickly to address the demand for a Bill of Rights. James Madison, who had initially been skeptical of the idea, took the lead in the First Congress. He culled through hundreds of suggestions from the state ratifying conventions and narrowed them down to twelve proposed amendments. Ten of these were ratified by the states and became the **Bill of Rights** in 1791.

> These amendments don't "grant" rights to the people. Instead, they use "negative" language to tell the government what it *cannot* do. This reinforces the principle that rights are inherent and that the government's power is limited.

The **First Amendment** is perhaps the most famous, protecting the core freedoms of expression: religion, speech, press, assembly, and petition. It prevents the government from establishing an official religion or interfering with the "free exercise" thereof.

The **Second Amendment** addresses the right to keep and bear arms, a provision rooted in the revolutionary fear of standing armies and the reliance on state militias.

The **Third and Fourth Amendments** protect the privacy and property of the individual. The Third prohibits the quartering of soldiers in private homes during peacetime, a direct response to British colonial practices. The Fourth protects against "unreasonable searches and seizures," requiring the government to show "probable cause" and obtain a warrant before invading a person's private space.

The **Fifth, Sixth, Seventh, and Eighth Amendments** focus on the rights of the accused and the legal process. They guarantee **due process**, protection against self-incrimination (the right to remain silent), the right to a speedy and public trial by an impartial jury, and the right to an attorney. The Eighth Amendment prohibits "excessive bail" and "cruel and unusual punishments," ensuring that the government's power to punish is not used as a tool of torture or political suppression.

The final two amendments are the most important for the structure of the government. The **Ninth Amendment** states that the listing of certain rights does not mean that the people do not have other rights that aren't listed. This was Madison's answer to Hamilton's fear that a Bill of Rights would be interpreted as a complete list. The **Tenth Amendment** reinforces the principle of federalism, stating that any powers not delegated to the federal government are "reserved to the States respectively, or to the people."

Incorporation Against the States

For the first century of American history, the Bill of Rights only applied to the federal government. This was confirmed by the Supreme Court in the 1833 case **Barron v. Baltimore**. Chief Justice John Marshall ruled that the amendments were intended to restrain the new national government, not the states. If a state government violated your freedom of speech or took your property without compensation, you could not look to the federal Bill of Rights for protection; you had to rely on your state constitution.

This changed after the Civil War with the passage of the **Fourteenth Amendment** in 1868. This amendment contains the **Due Process Clause**, which states:

> "nor shall any State deprive any person of life, liberty, or property, without due process of law."

Starting in the early twentieth century, the Supreme Court began a process known as **selective incorporation**. The Court interpreted the word "liberty" in the Fourteenth Amendment to include many of the fundamental rights listed in the first ten amendments. One by one, the Court applied these federal protections to the state governments.

In **Gitlow v. New York** (1925), the Court incorporated freedom of speech. In **Near v. Minnesota** (1931), it incorporated freedom of the press. In **Mapp v. Ohio** (1961), it applied the Fourth Amendment's protection against illegal searches to the states. In **Gideon v. Wainwright** (1963), it required states to provide attorneys for poor defendants in criminal cases. In **McDonald v. Chicago** (2010), the Court incorporated the Second Amendment's right to bear arms.

Today, almost all the major protections of the Bill of Rights apply to both federal and state governments. This has fundamentally shifted the power dynamic of the country. It has made the federal courts the ultimate guardians of individual liberty, allowing them to strike down state laws that infringe on constitutional rights. While some "originalists" argue that this goes beyond the intent of the Founders, incorporation has become a central pillar of modern American law.

Subsequent Constitutional Amendments

The amendment process defined in Article V has been used seventeen times since the Bill of Rights was added. These amendments generally fall into three categories: expanding the right to vote, refining government procedures, and correcting fundamental injustices.

The **Civil War Amendments** (13th, 14th, and 15th) represented a "second founding." The Thirteenth Amendment abolished slavery. The Fourteenth Amendment established national citizenship and guaranteed equal protection under the law. The Fifteenth Amendment prohibited denying the right to vote based on race. These amendments fundamentally altered the relationship between the federal government and the states, giving Congress the power to intervene in state affairs to protect civil rights.

The **Progressive Era Amendments** (16th, 17th, 18th, and 19th) reflected a desire for social and political reform. The Sixteenth Amendment allowed for a federal income tax, giving the government a massive new source of revenue. The Seventeenth Amendment provided for the **direct election of senators** by the people, rather than by state legislatures. The Eighteenth Amendment began the failed experiment of Prohibition, which was later repealed by the Twenty-first Amendment. The Nineteenth Amendment finally guaranteed women the right to vote.

Several amendments have addressed the mechanics of the Presidency. The **Twenty-second Amendment** limited presidents to two terms in office, codifying the tradition started by George Washington. The **Twenty-fifth Amendment** clarified the process for presidential succession and established a procedure for dealing with a president who becomes incapacitated.

The most recent amendments have focused on expanding the electorate. The **Twenty-fourth Amendment** abolished poll taxes, which were used in many Southern states to prevent Black citizens from voting. The **Twenty-sixth Amendment**, ratified during the Vietnam War, lowered the voting age from 21 to 18, based on the argument that if people were old enough to be drafted and die for their country, they were old enough to vote.

The final amendment, the **Twenty-seventh**, has one of the strangest histories in American law. It prohibits Congress from giving itself a pay raise that takes effect before the next election. It was originally proposed by James Madison in 1789 as part of the original Bill of Rights but failed to get enough state support. In the 1980s, a college student discovered that the amendment had no expiration date and began a campaign to get it ratified. It finally became part of the Constitution in 1992, over 200 years after it was written.

The history of ratification and the ongoing amendment process proves that the Constitution is not a static document. It is a living framework that has been shaped by debate, conflict, and the changing values of the American people. The Federalists won the argument for a strong central government, but the Anti-Federalists won the argument for a Bill of Rights. This tension, between the need for an effective government and the need to protect individual freedom, remains the driving force of the American political experiment. Each amendment represents a moment where the nation decided to re-examine its foundational rules to reflect a "more perfect union."

The ratification battle also established the precedent of public debate as a vital part of governance. The Federalist Papers were attempts to persuade the common citizen. This tradition of open, vigorous, and often partisan debate continues to define the American democratic process. While the actors and the issues have changed, the fundamental questions about the limits of federal power and the scope of individual rights are the same ones that were debated in the statehouses of 1788.

One could argue that the Anti-Federalists were the most successful "losers" in history. Their skepticism forced the Federalists to build a better, more accountable system. Demanding the Bill of Rights, they committed to the idea that the American government would be defined as much by what it cannot do as by what it can. The resulting document is a delicate balance of authority and liberty, a structure that has survived for over two centuries because it’s strong enough to lead but flexible enough to change.

Do you think the Anti-Federalists' fear that the "Necessary and Proper Clause" would lead to an unlimited expansion of federal power has been proven right by modern American history?

Chapter 5: Federalism and the Division of Power

Federalism defines the American political identity as a system of shared sovereignty. It isn't a mere administrative convenience; it is a structural barrier against the centralization of power. While the Constitution's first three articles separate power horizontally among the legislative, executive, and judicial branches, federalism divides power vertically between the national government and the states. This arrangement creates a constant, healthy friction that forces both levels of government to justify their actions and protect their respective jurisdictions.

The United States was the first nation to successfully implement this model on a continental scale. Previous republics were either small city-states or loose confederations that lacked a central authority capable of maintaining order. The Founders rejected the unitary system of Great Britain, where all power flowed from the top down, and the confederal system of the Articles of Confederation, where power remained entirely with the states. They chose instead a middle path that recognizes two distinct spheres of authority, each operating directly on the citizens within the same territory.

The Supremacy Clause: The Legal Anchor

Every federal system needs a rule for resolving conflicts. Without a final arbiter, the national government and the states would eventually paralyze each other.

The Constitution provides this rule in Article VI, Clause 2, commonly known as the **Supremacy Clause**. It establishes a clear hierarchy: the Constitution, federal laws made in accordance with the Constitution, and all treaties are the "supreme Law of the Land."

This clause doesn’t give the federal government unlimited power. It only applies when the federal government acts within its delegated authority. If Congress passes a law that falls outside its enumerated or implied powers, that law is not supreme because it is unconstitutional. However, when a valid federal law conflicts with a state law, the state law must give way. This principle ensures that the United States functions as a single legal entity rather than a patchwork of fifty different sets of rules on matters of national importance.

The Supreme Court reinforced this hierarchy in the 1819 case **McCulloch v. Maryland**. When Maryland attempted to tax the Second Bank of the United States, Chief Justice John Marshall ruled that "the power to tax involves the power to destroy." He argued that if states could tax federal institutions, they could effectively nullify federal authority. The Supremacy Clause prevents states from using their reserved powers to undermine the national government's ability to carry out its constitutional duties.

In the modern era, the Supremacy Clause is the basis for **preemption**. When the federal government chooses to regulate an entire field, such as aviation safety or nuclear energy, it "preempts" any state regulations in that area. Even if a state law is more stringent than a federal law, it may be struck down if it interferes with a uniform national standard. This legal mechanism maintains the integrity of the internal market and ensures that federal policy isn't fragmented by local politics.

Reserved Powers of the States

While the federal government is limited to its enumerated powers, the states possess a broad, residual authority. The **Tenth Amendment** clarifies this relationship by stating that "the powers not delegated to the United States by the Constitution, nor prohibited by it to the States, are reserved to the States respectively, or to the people."

These are known as **Reserved Powers**.

The most significant of these is the **police power**. This isn't just about law enforcement, but the inherent authority of a state to regulate for the health, safety, welfare, and morals of its citizens. This power is the reason most aspects of your daily life are governed by state law rather than federal law. The states manage public education, establish marriage and divorce laws, regulate intrastate commerce, and oversee the licensing of professionals like doctors and lawyers.

States also serve as "laboratories of democracy," a phrase coined by Justice Louis Brandeis. Because each state has its own reserved powers, it can experiment with new social and economic policies without involving the entire nation. If a policy fails in one state, the damage is localized. If it succeeds, other states and even the federal government can adopt it. Examples of this process include women's suffrage, which began in Western states long before the 19th Amendment, and modern healthcare reforms that started at the state level.

The boundary of reserved powers is often defined by what the federal government is prohibited from doing. For instance, the federal government cannot command state officials to carry out federal regulatory programs. This is the **anti-commandeering doctrine**, established in cases like *Printz v. United States* (1997). The Court ruled that Congress could not require local sheriffs to perform background checks on handgun purchasers. Even when the federal government has a legitimate goal, it cannot treat state governments as its administrative subordinates.

Concurrent Powers

Not all powers belong exclusively to one level of government. **Concurrent Powers** are those shared by both the federal government and the states. These powers are exercised simultaneously within the same territory and over the same population. This overlap is a practical necessity; both levels of government must be able to perform certain basic functions to remain viable.

The most prominent concurrent power is the **power to tax**. You likely pay both federal and state income taxes, and you pay sales taxes to the state while the federal government levies excise taxes on specific goods like gasoline or tobacco. Both levels of government must have the ability to raise revenue independently to fund their operations. If one level were dependent on the other for its budget, the dependent level would lose its sovereignty.

Other examples of concurrent powers include:

- **Establishing Courts -** There is a complete federal court system and fifty separate state court systems.
- **Borrowing Money -** Both the U.S. Treasury and state governments can issue bonds to fund infrastructure or manage debt.
- **Making and Enforcing Laws -** A single act, such as a bank robbery or a drug sale, can violate both federal and state laws, leading to prosecutions in both jurisdictions.
- **Building Infrastructure -** Federal and state governments collaborate on the interstate highway system, though each maintains its own roads and bridges.
- **Promoting General Welfare -** Both levels of government fund public health initiatives and social safety nets.

Concurrent powers create a complex web of governance. While they allow for flexibility, they also lead to jurisdictional disputes. When both levels of government regulate the same activity, the Supremacy Clause determines which law takes precedence in the event of a direct conflict. Nonetheless in many cases, the two levels cooperate through shared funding and joint task forces, blurring the lines of responsibility.

Dual Federalism: The Layer Cake Model

From the founding of the republic until the 1930s, the dominant view was **Dual Federalism**. This model envisions the national government and the states as co-equal sovereigns, each supreme within its own clearly defined sphere. Political scientists often call this "layer cake federalism" because the levels of government are distinct and do not overlap.

Under dual federalism, the federal government stuck strictly to its enumerated powers: national defense, foreign policy, coining money, and regulating interstate commerce. The states handled everything else, including property law, civil rights, and social welfare.

The Supreme Court acted as the umpire, ensuring that neither level encroached on the other's territory. During this era, the Court often used the Tenth Amendment to strike down federal laws that it felt invaded the states' reserved powers.

A classic example of dual federalism in action was the case of **Hammer v. Dagenhart** (1918). Congress tried to ban child labor by prohibiting the interstate shipment of goods produced by children. The Supreme Court struck the law down, arguing that the regulation of manufacturing was a local matter reserved for the states. The Court maintained that the commerce power could not be used as a "pretext" to regulate social conditions that were traditionally under state control.

This rigid separation eventually collapsed under the weight of the Great Depression. The economic crisis was so vast and systemic that state governments were overwhelmed. They lacked the resources to provide relief to millions of unemployed citizens. The American public began to demand national solutions to national problems, leading to a fundamental shift in the federal-state relationship.

Cooperative Federalism: The Marble Cake Model

The New Deal programs of Franklin D. Roosevelt ushered in the era of **Cooperative Federalism**. This model replaced the "layer cake" with a "marble cake," where the responsibilities of the federal and state governments are intermingled. Instead of working in separate spheres, the two levels of government began to work together to solve complex problems.

The primary mechanism of cooperative federalism is the **grant-in-aid**. This occurs when the federal government provides funding to the states to implement specific programs. These grants allowed the federal government to influence policy areas that were technically reserved to the states, such as education and transportation. By offering money, the federal government could "encourage" states to adopt national standards without directly violating the Tenth Amendment.

Type of Grant	Definition	Flexibility
Categorical Grant	Money provided for a specific, narrowly defined purpose (e.g., school lunches).	Low; states must follow strict federal rules.
Block Grant	Money provided for a broad functional area (e.g., community development).	High; states have discretion on how to spend it.
Formula Grant	Distributed based on a mathematical formula (e.g., census data or poverty levels).	Automatic; based on qualifying criteria.

Cooperative federalism transformed the federal government into the senior partner in the relationship. While states still administered many programs, the federal government provided the funding and set the guidelines. The Social Security Act of 1935 is a prime example; it created a national system of old-age insurance while providing federal matching funds for state-run unemployment and disability programs.

This era also saw the expansion of the **Commerce Clause**. The Supreme Court began to rule that almost any economic activity, no matter how local, had a "substantial effect" on interstate commerce. In *Wickard v. Filburn* (1942), the Court ruled that the federal government could regulate a farmer growing wheat for his own use because his actions, when aggregated with others, affected the national market. This interpretation effectively gave the federal government the power to regulate almost every aspect of the economy, further eroding the distinctions of dual federalism.

Fiscal Federalism and Mandates

The relationship today is often described as **Fiscal Federalism**, a subset of the cooperative model that focuses on the power of the purse. The federal government uses its massive tax revenue to shape state policy through conditions of aid. If a state wants federal highway funds, it must agree to a national minimum drinking age of twenty-one.

This was upheld in **South Dakota v. Dole** (1987), where the Court ruled that Congress can use its spending power to indirectly influence state policy, as long as the conditions are clear and related to the national interest.

However, this influence can become coercive. **Unfunded Mandates** occur when the federal government requires states to perform certain actions but provides no money to pay for them. The Clean Air Act and the Americans with Disabilities Act are examples where states must meet expensive federal standards using their own tax dollars. While the Unfunded Mandates Reform Act of 1995 attempted to limit this practice, it remains a major source of tension between state governors and the federal government.

Mandates highlight the darker side of cooperative federalism. While cooperation implies a partnership, the reality is often "coercive federalism," where the federal government uses its financial leverage to force states to comply with national priorities. This has led to a push for **Devolution**, the effort to return more power and responsibility to the states. This movement gained momentum in the 1990s with welfare reform, which turned many federal programs into block grants and gave states more control over eligibility and work requirements.

Federalism as a Shield and a Sword

The division of power remains one of the most litigated and debated aspects of the American system. In recent years, the Supreme Court has signaled a renewed interest in protecting the "dignity" of the states.

Cases like **United States v. Lopez** (1995) and **United States v. Morrison** (2000) struck down federal laws for the first time in sixty years on the grounds that they exceeded the commerce power and invaded state territory.

Yet, federalism is also used by states to resist federal policy. "Sanctuary cities" and states that have legalized marijuana in defiance of federal law are modern examples of states using their reserved powers and local autonomy to challenge national authority. Conversely, the federal government uses its supremacy to protect civil rights when states fail to do so, as seen during the Civil Rights Movement of the 1960s.

Federalism ensures that no single majority can dominate the entire country. It forces a diverse nation to find a balance between national unity and local diversity. While the line between federal and state power shifts over time, the existence of the line itself is what prevents the United States from becoming a centralized autocracy. The "marble cake" may be messy, but it reflects the reality of a complex, continental republic where power is never settled, only negotiated.

The division of power also complicates the political process. Because different levels of government control different things, it can be difficult for citizens to know whom to hold accountable when things go wrong. When a natural disaster strikes, is the failure the fault of the local mayor, the state governor, or the federal emergency agency? This ambiguity is the price of a system designed to frustrate the easy exercise of power.

The Supremacy Clause provides the final word, but the Tenth Amendment provides the recurring question. The tug-of-war between these two constitutional poles is the heartbeat of American governance. It ensures that the debate over who has the authority to act is never truly finished, requiring every generation to re-examine the foundations of their liberty.

Does the modern shift toward "coercive federalism," where the federal government uses funding to force state compliance, undermine the original intent of the Tenth Amendment as a protection for state sovereignty?

Chapter 6: Separation of Powers and Checks and Balances

If the Constitution provides the skeleton of the American government, the system of separation of powers acts as its nervous system, constantly regulating and balancing the impulses of each branch.

The Founders didn't trust human nature. They operated under the assumption that anyone given power would eventually seek to expand it. To prevent the concentration of authority in a single set of hands, they designed a government where the branches are not only separate but also inherently competitive.

This isn't an efficient system by design. It creates a deliberate friction that forces compromise and slows the pace of governance. The goal wasn't to create a government that could act quickly, but one that couldn't act tyrannically. By dividing the power to make, enforce, and interpret laws, the Framers ensured that no single faction could dominate the nation without the broad and sustained consent of the governed.

Madisonian Theory of Factions

James Madison arrived at the Constitutional Convention with a specific problem in mind: the "mischiefs of faction." In **Federalist No. 10**, he defined a **faction** as a group of citizens, whether a majority or a minority, united by a common passion or interest that is adverse to the rights of other citizens or the permanent interests of the community. He viewed factions as an inevitable byproduct of liberty. Just as air fuels fire, liberty fuels factions. You can't abolish them without destroying the very freedom the government is supposed to protect.

Madison's solution wasn't to remove the causes of factions but to control their effects. He argued that in a small society, a majority faction can easily coordinate to oppress a minority. However, in a large, "extended republic" like the United States, the sheer diversity of interests makes it difficult for a single majority to form. Farmers, merchants, creditors, debtors, and members of various religious sects all compete for influence. This fragmentation ensures that a majority must be a coalition of many different groups, which naturally moderates their demands.

In **Federalist No. 51**, Madison explained how the structure of the government itself would safeguard liberty. He famously wrote, "If men were angels, no government would be necessary. If angels were to govern men, neither external nor internal controls on government would be necessary." Since neither is true, the government must be designed so that "ambition must be made to counteract ambition."

The **Madisonian Model** separates the government into three branches: the legislative, executive, and judicial. Madison recognized that a mere "parchment barrier" (a written statement saying the branches are separate) wouldn't be enough. Each branch needs the constitutional means and the personal motives to resist encroachments from the others. Connecting the "interest of the man" with the "constitutional rights of the place," the system uses the human desire for power as a tool for stability.

This theory assumes that the President will want to protect executive authority, members of Congress will want to protect legislative prerogatives, and judges will want to protect their independence. When the executive branch tries to overreach, the legislature has an incentive to stop it, not just out of virtue, but to preserve its own influence. The system turns a potential vice (ambition) into a public benefit.

Legislative Checks on the Executive

The Framers viewed the legislature as the most potentially dangerous branch because it holds the power to create the law. Consequently, they gave it the most robust set of checks on the other branches. The legislative branch doesn't just pass bills; it serves as a constant monitor of executive activity.

The **power of the purse** is the most significant legislative check. Article I, Section 9, Clause 7 states that "No Money shall be drawn from the Treasury, but in Consequence of Appropriations made by Law." This means the President cannot spend a single dime that Congress hasn't authorized. If Congress disagrees with an executive agency's actions or a President's military venture, it can simply withhold funding. This financial leverage gives Congress the final word on the scope and scale of every executive initiative.

Impeachment serves as the "ultimate" check, reserved for the most serious abuses of power. The House of Representatives has the sole power to impeach (charge) the President or other civil officers for "Treason, Bribery, or other high Crimes and Misdemeanors." If the House impeaches, the Senate conducts a trial presided over by the Chief Justice. A two-thirds vote in the Senate is required for conviction and removal from office.

Impeachment Phase	Body Responsible	Vote Required	Result
Impeachment (Indictment)	House of Representatives	Simple Majority	Formal charges are filed
Trial	Senate	N/A	Evidence and arguments presented

Conviction/ Removal	Senate	Two-Thirds (67 votes)	Immediate removal from office

The Senate also holds the power of **Advice and Consent**. The President can negotiate treaties and appoint ambassadors, cabinet members, and federal judges, but none of these actions are final until the Senate approves them. Treaties require a two-thirds vote, while appointments require a simple majority. This ensures that the President cannot fill the government with cronies or bind the nation to international agreements without the support of the states' representatives.

Congressional oversight and investigation allow the legislature to look into the executive branch's "back office." Congress holds hearings, subpoenas documents, and questions officials to ensure laws are being executed properly and money is being spent as intended. While the Constitution doesn't explicitly mention oversight, the Supreme Court has ruled it's an implied power essential to the lawmaking process. When a scandal erupts in an executive agency, it is usually a congressional committee that brings it to light.

Finally, Congress holds the **War Powers**. While the President is the Commander in Chief of the armed forces, only Congress has the power to declare war and raise an army. This was intended to prevent a single person from dragging the nation into unnecessary conflicts.

The **War Powers Resolution of 1973** attempted to clarify this relationship, requiring the President to notify Congress within 48 hours of deploying troops and to withdraw them within 60 days unless Congress authorizes the action.

Executive Checks on the Legislature

The President isn't a passive observer of the legislative process. The executive branch has several mechanisms to prevent Congress from becoming too powerful or passing laws that the President deems unwise or unconstitutional.

The primary check is the **Veto Power**. Every bill passed by the House and the Senate must be presented to the President. If the President signs it, it becomes law. If the President returns it with objections, it's a veto. This gives the President a seat at the legislative table, as the mere threat of a veto can force Congress to modify a bill's contents to suit executive preferences.

The President also influences the legislative agenda through the **State of the Union** address. Article II, Section 3 requires the President to "from time to time give to the Congress Information of the State of the Union, and recommend to their Consideration such Measures as he shall judge necessary and expedient." While the President can't formally introduce a bill, the executive branch drafts much of the legislation that Congress considers, using the "bully pulpit" of the presidency to build public support and pressure lawmakers.

In extreme circumstances, the President has the power to **convene or adjourn Congress**. If the House and Senate cannot agree on a time to adjourn, the President can step in and set a date. The President can also call Congress into "special session" during a national emergency. While rarely used today, these powers emphasize that the executive is a co-equal participant in the timing of governance.

The President's power to **appoint judges** is a significant, albeit indirect, check on the legislature. Choosing individuals with a specific judicial philosophy, the President can influence how the courts interpret the laws Congress passes. If a President appoints judges who favor a narrow interpretation of federal power, they may strike down congressional acts that they view as overstepping constitutional boundaries.

Executive Orders and directives represent a "soft" check. While these aren't mentioned in the Constitution, they allow the President to manage the operations of the federal government. If Congress passes a vague law, the President uses executive orders to determine how that law is implemented on the ground. In some cases, Presidents use these orders to bypass a gridlocked Congress, though the courts can strike them down if they cross the line into actual lawmaking.

Veto and Override Mechanisms

The veto process is a perfect example of the "deliberate friction" inherent in the American system. It isn't an absolute power, but a qualified one. It requires the President to take a public stand and provide a written justification for rejecting a bill.

When a bill arrives on the President's desk, he has ten days (excluding Sundays) to act. He has four options:

1. **Sign the bill:** It becomes law.
2. **Veto the bill:** He sends it back to the chamber where it originated with a "veto message" explaining his reasons.
3. **Allow it to become law without a signature:** If he does nothing for ten days and Congress is still in session, the bill becomes law anyway. This is often done when a President dislikes a bill but knows a veto would be overridden.
4. **The Pocket Veto:** If the President does nothing for ten days and Congress adjourns during that period, the bill dies. This is "putting the bill in his pocket." Unlike a regular veto, a pocket veto cannot be overridden because Congress is no longer in session to vote on it.

To **override a veto**, Congress must pass the bill again with a **two-thirds majority** in both the House and the Senate. This is an intentionally high bar. It ensures that a law can only be enacted over the President's objection if there is overwhelming national consensus. In the history of the United States, only about 7% of presidential vetoes have been successfully overridden.

Veto Type	Action Taken	Can it be Overridden?	Condition

Regular Veto	President returns bill with objections	Yes	Requires 2/3 vote in both houses
Pocket Veto	President ignores bill; Congress adjourns	No	Congress must be out of session

The veto serves as a shield for the executive branch and a check on what Hamilton called the "legislative vortex." Without it, Congress could pass laws that strip the President of his constitutional duties or target specific individuals. It forces the two branches to negotiate. Often, a "veto threat" is more effective than an actual veto, as it brings congressional leaders to the White House to hammer out a compromise before the bill is even finalized.

Judicial Review

The most powerful check in the American system isn't explicitly mentioned in the Constitution. **Judicial Review** is the power of the courts to declare acts of Congress, actions of the President, or state laws unconstitutional. This authority makes the Supreme Court the final arbiter of what the Constitution means.

In the early years of the republic, the judicial branch was seen as the "least dangerous" branch because it possessed neither the "purse" nor the "sword." It couldn't raise money and it couldn't enforce its own rulings. That changed in 1803 with the landmark case of **Marbury v. Madison**.

The case involved William Marbury, who had been appointed as a justice of the peace by outgoing President John Adams. The new Secretary of State, James Madison, refused to deliver the commission. Marbury sued, asking the Supreme Court to issue a "writ of mandamus" to force the delivery.

Chief Justice **John Marshall** found himself in a political trap. If he ordered the commission delivered, the Jefferson administration would likely ignore him, making the Court look weak. If he refused, it would look like he was caving to political pressure.

Marshall's solution was a stroke of judicial genius. He ruled that while Marbury was entitled to his commission, the law that gave the Supreme Court the power to issue the writ (the Judiciary Act of 1789) was unconstitutional. By striking down a law passed by Congress, Marshall established the principle that "It is emphatically the province and duty of the judicial department to say what the law is."

Judicial review ensures that the Constitution remains the supreme law of the land. If the legislature passes a law that violates the Bill of Rights, the Court can strike it down. If the President issues an executive order that exceeds his authority, the Court can nullify it. This provides a vital protection for minority rights against the "tyranny of the majority." Since federal judges are appointed for life, they can make unpopular decisions without fear of losing their jobs in the next election.

(Marshall's deeper contribution was procedural: he positioned the Court as a co-equal branch by embedding judicial review within the act of deciding cases, not as a political claim. He made constitutional interpretation an unavoidable function of judging itself, ensuring the power would persist without needing explicit constitutional enumeration.)

However, judicial review also creates a paradox. In a democracy, the ultimate power is supposed to rest with the people. Yet, the final word on the most important legal and social issues is held by nine unelected, life-tenured judges. This has led to recurring debates over **judicial activism** (where judges are accused of making policy from the bench) versus **judicial restraint** (where judges defer to the elected branches whenever possible).

The other branches have checks on the judiciary as well. Congress determines the size of the Supreme Court and can create or abolish lower courts. If the Court makes a decision that Congress dislikes, it can attempt to pass a constitutional amendment to effectively "overrule" the Court, as happened with the 16th Amendment (income tax) and the 26th Amendment (voting age). The President's power to appoint judges ensures that the Court eventually reflects the political shifts of the nation, even if it takes decades for those changes to manifest.

The System in Motion

Separation of powers and checks and balances aren't just dry legal concepts; they are the mechanics of American political conflict. You see them in action during every budget showdown, every Supreme Court confirmation hearing, and every debate over executive overreach.

The system is designed to prevent any one branch from becoming too efficient. Efficiency in government is often the enemy of liberty. If a President could simply decree a law, the government would move much faster, but there would be no protection against a bad or biased decree. By requiring the House to agree with the Senate, and the President to agree with both, and the Courts to find the result consistent with the Constitution, the system is designed so that only policies with broad support become permanent.

This "interlocking" nature of power means that the branches are constantly in a state of negotiation. It creates a government of **shared powers** rather than strictly separated ones. The President participates in the legislative process through the veto; Congress participates in the executive process through oversight and the power of the purse; the Courts participate in both through interpretation.

The Madisonian theory has largely succeeded in its goal. While the power of the presidency has grown significantly over the last century, the system of checks still functions. The legislature still controls the budget, the courts still strike down executive actions, and the threat of impeachment still looms over the Oval Office. The "ambition" of each branch continues to act as a hedge against the others.

The greatest challenge to this system today isn't the strength of one branch, but the rise of intense **partisan polarization**. When members of Congress value their party loyalty more than their institutional loyalty, the Madisonian check weakens.

If a majority in Congress refuses to check a President of their own party, the "ambition" of the legislature no longer counteracts the "ambition" of the executive. In such times, the burden of maintaining the balance shifts increasingly to the judicial branch and the voters themselves.

The Founders didn't expect the government to be harmonious. They expected it to be a scene of constant competition. They didn't want a "team" working together; they wanted a set of rivals watching each other. This rivalry is the primary safeguard of the American republic. As long as each branch remains jealous of its own power, the liberty of the individual remains secure. The friction of the system is the sound of democracy working.

Does the modern trend of "government by executive order" suggest that the legislative branch has become too willing to cede its power to the President, thereby breaking the Madisonian balance?

Chapter 7: The Legislative Branch

The first article of the Constitution focuses entirely on the legislative branch. This placement is no accident. The Framers believed that in a representative republic, the power to make laws should be the preeminent authority. They intended for Congress to be the most responsive to the people and the most capable of checking the other two branches. Granting the legislature the first position in the founding document, the authors established a clear hierarchy: the people's representatives hold the primary responsibility for determining the nation's path.

Bicameralism and Its Rationale

The United States Congress consists of two separate chambers: the House of Representatives and the Senate. This **bicameral** structure reflects a fundamental compromise between competing visions of democracy and state sovereignty. At the Constitutional Convention, the debate over representation nearly destroyed the young nation. Small states demanded an equal vote for every state, while large states insisted that representation should reflect the number of citizens. The resulting "Great Compromise" created the two-chamber system we use today.

Bicameralism serves a purpose far beyond political compromise. It functions as an internal check on the legislative power itself. The Framers understood that a single, all-powerful legislature could become just as tyrannical as a monarch.

Dividing the branch into two bodies with different constituencies, terms of office, and institutional cultures, they created a system where passing a law would be a difficult, deliberate process. Every bill must survive the scrutiny of both the "People's House" and the "State's House" before it reaches the President's desk.

James Madison described the necessity of this division in *Federalist No. 51*. He argued that in a republican government, the legislative authority necessarily predominates. To remedy this "inconvenience," the government must divide the legislature into different branches and render them, by different modes of election and different principles of action, as little connected with each other as the nature of their common functions and their common dependence on the society will admit.

A popular, albeit perhaps apocryphal, story involves George Washington and Thomas Jefferson discussing this very structure. Jefferson supposedly asked why the convention had created a second chamber. Washington asked Jefferson why he poured his coffee into his saucer before drinking it. When Jefferson replied that he did so to cool it, Washington noted that the Senate serves a similar function: it "cools" the hot-headed passions of the more populist House of Representatives.

This system guarantees that no faction can easily sweep a radical agenda through the government in a single election cycle. Because the House and Senate represent different interests, they often disagree on the details of policy. This disagreement forces negotiation and moderation. While critics often complain about legislative gridlock, the Framers viewed this slowing of the process as a essential protection for the rights of the minority.

House of Representatives Composition

The Constitution describes the House of Representatives as the chamber most closely tied to the will of the people. To ensure this connection, members face reelection every two years. This frequent cycle keeps representatives on a short leash, forcing them to remain attentive to the shifting moods and needs of their constituents.

The number of representatives is based on **apportionment**, the process of dividing the seats among the states according to their population. The Constitution requires a national census every ten years to determine these numbers accurately.

Originally, the House was quite small: the first Congress had only 65 members. As the nation expanded, the House grew until it reached 435 members in 1911. The **Permanent Apportionment Act of 1929** fixed the number of seats at 435 to prevent the chamber from becoming too large to function.

Each state is guaranteed at least one representative, regardless of its population. Beyond that minimum, seats are distributed using a mathematical formula that ensures relatively equal representation across state lines. Currently, the average representative speaks for roughly 760,000 people. This massive constituency size has changed the nature of representation since the founding, when the ratio was roughly one representative for every 30,000 citizens.

The House is often called "The People's House" because it was the only part of the federal government originally elected directly by the people. This direct link gives the House a unique democratic legitimacy. It is the chamber where the most diverse range of views and backgrounds usually appears. Because representatives serve small districts rather than entire states, they often focus on local issues and the specific economic interests of their neighbors.

Leadership in the House is highly centralized. The **Speaker of the House**, an office specifically mentioned in the Constitution, holds immense power over the legislative agenda. Because the House is so large, it requires strict rules to maintain order. Debate is often limited, and the majority party generally exercises tight control over which bills reach the floor for a vote. This efficiency stands in stark contrast to the more deliberative, and often slower, Senate.

Senate Composition

The Senate represents the states as political entities rather than the population as individuals. Every state, from California to Wyoming, has exactly two senators. This equal representation was a non-negotiable demand of the smaller states during the Constitutional Convention. It ensures that the interests of less populous regions are not steamrolled by the massive populations of urban centers.

Originally, state legislatures chose their senators. The Framers believed this would insulate the Senate from popular passions and make sure that senators remained loyal to the interests of their state governments. But this often led to corruption and prolonged vacancies when state legislatures could not agree on a candidate. The **17th Amendment**, ratified in 1913, changed this system to allow for the direct election of senators by the people of each state.

Senators serve six-year terms, the longest of any elected officials in the federal government. To provide stability, these terms are staggered. Only one-third of the Senate is up for reelection every two years. This "continuous body" structure means that at any given time, two-thirds of the Senate consists of experienced members who are not currently focused on a campaign. This design encourages senators to take a longer-term view of national policy.

The Vice President of the United States serves as the **President of the Senate**, but they hold no legislative power and only vote to break a tie. The day-to-day operations are usually handled by the **President Pro Tempore** (typically the most senior member of the majority party) and the Senate Majority Leader.

Unlike the House, the Senate operates under rules that emphasize the rights of individual members. Any single senator can often slow down or block legislation through various procedural maneuvers, including the filibuster.

The Senate's role in the federal system is more prestigious and expansive than that of the House. It holds the unique power of "Advice and Consent" over presidential appointments and treaties. A senator represents an entire state, which typically requires them to appeal to a broader and more moderate coalition of voters than a representative from a small, specialized district. This statewide perspective often makes the Senate a more deliberative and cautious body.

Qualifications and Terms of Office

The Constitution sets specific, modest qualifications for serving in Congress. The Framers wanted to keep the path to office open to a wide range of citizens, but they also wanted to ensure that lawmakers possessed a certain level of maturity and a stake in the nation's future.

For the **House of Representatives**, a candidate must:

- Be at least 25 years old.
- Have been a citizen of the United States for at least seven years.
- Be an inhabitant of the state they represent at the time of the election.

For the **Senate**, the requirements are slightly higher, reflecting the chamber's intended role as a more "mature" body:

- Be at least 30 years old.
- Have been a citizen of the United States for at least nine years.
- Be an inhabitant of the state they represent at the time of the election.

The residency requirement was intended to prevent "carpetbagging," the practice of moving to a new area specifically to run for office. Interestingly, the Constitution does not require a representative to live within the specific district they represent, only within the state. Custom and political reality usually dictate that they live in the district, but the legal requirement is broader.

The difference in term lengths, two years for the House versus six years for the Senate, creates two very different political environments. House members are essentially in a state of permanent campaign. They must constantly raise money and visit their districts to maintain their support. This makes them highly responsive but also prone to short-term thinking.

Senators, with their six-year terms, have the luxury of "cooling off" between elections. They can support unpopular but necessary policies early in their terms, betting that the public will have forgotten the controversy by the time they face the voters again.

The lack of **term limits** is one of the most debated aspects of the legislative branch. While the President is limited to two terms by the 22nd Amendment, representatives and senators can serve as long as the voters continue to reelect them. Some argue that this leads to a "permanent political class" out of touch with regular citizens. Others contend that seniority and experience are vital for navigating the complex legislative process and checking the power of the executive branch and professional lobbyists.

Constitutional Powers of Congress

Article I, Section 8 is the heart of congressional authority. It contains the **enumerated powers**, a specific list of responsibilities that the federal government possesses. If a power is not on this list (or implied by it), the federal government technically cannot exercise it. This list was designed to solve the problems of the Articles of Confederation by giving the central government the tools it needed to function as a sovereign nation.

The **Power to Tax and Spend** is the most significant of these authorities. Congress can "lay and collect Taxes, Duties, Imposts and Excises" to pay the debts and provide for the common defense and general welfare.

This gives Congress control over the national economy and the ability to fund every other government function. All bills for raising revenue must originate in the House of Representatives, ensuring that the body closest to the taxpayers has the first word on how their money is taken.

The **Commerce Clause** allows Congress to "regulate Commerce with foreign Nations, and among the several States." While this originally meant regulating the physical transport of goods across state lines, the Supreme Court has interpreted this power broadly. Today, it serves as the legal basis for everything from environmental regulations to civil rights laws and federal drug prohibitions. Almost any activity that has a "substantial effect" on the national economy falls under this congressional umbrella.

Congress also holds the **War Powers**. While the President is the Commander in Chief, only Congress can formally declare war. It also has the power to "raise and support Armies" and "provide and maintain a Navy." By giving the power of the sword to the branch that controls the purse, the Framers ensured that the President could not easily wage war without the ongoing support of the people's representatives.

Other specific enumerated powers include:

- **Borrowing money** on the credit of the United States.
- Establishing uniform rules for **naturalization** and **bankruptcies**.
- **Coining money** and regulating its value.
- Providing for the punishment of **counterfeiting**.
- Establishing **post offices** and post roads.
- Promoting the progress of science and useful arts through **patents and copyrights**.
- Creating **federal courts** below the Supreme Court.
- Defining and punishing **piracies and felonies** committed on the high seas.
- Exercising exclusive legislation over the **District of Columbia**.

The final clause of Section 8 is the **Necessary and Proper Clause**. It grants Congress the power to "make all Laws which shall be necessary and proper for carrying into Execution the foregoing Powers." This is the foundation of the government's implied authority, allowing Congress to adapt its specific powers to changing circumstances.

Enumerated versus Implied Authority

The tension between enumerated and implied powers is the central conflict of American constitutional law. An **enumerated power** is one explicitly stated in the text. For example, the Constitution says Congress can "establish Post Offices." This is clear and unambiguous. However, the world is more complex than a list of eighteen bullet points. To be effective, a government must be able to take actions that are logical extensions of its written powers.

Implied powers are those not specifically mentioned but deemed necessary to carry out the enumerated ones. The **Necessary and Proper Clause** acts as the legal bridge. For instance, the Constitution does not explicitly give Congress the power to create a national bank. However, in the landmark case *McCulloch v. Maryland* (1819), the Supreme Court ruled that because Congress has the enumerated powers to tax, borrow money, and regulate commerce, creating a bank is a "necessary and proper" way to manage those financial responsibilities.

This "Elastic Clause" has allowed the federal government to expand far beyond the vision of the 1787 Drafters.

- The power to regulate interstate commerce implies the power to regulate the internet, television broadcasts, and airline safety.

- The power to collect taxes implies the power to create the Internal Revenue Service (IRS).
- The power to raise an army implies the power to institute a military draft.

Critics of this expansion, often called **strict constructionists**, argue that the federal government should only do what is literally written in the text. They fear that a broad interpretation of implied powers eventually makes the Tenth Amendment (which reserves powers to the states) meaningless. If "necessary and proper" can be interpreted to mean "convenient or useful," then there is essentially no limit to federal authority.

On the other side, **loose constructionists** argue that the Constitution is a "living document" that must evolve. They point out that a government that cannot adapt to the industrial revolution, the nuclear age, or the digital era would quickly become obsolete. They believe the Framers used broad language like "general welfare" and "necessary and proper" precisely because they knew they could not predict the future.

This debate determines the reality of American life. Every time Congress passes a major new piece of legislation (whether it's the Affordable Care Act, a new environmental regulation, or a national security law) the courts must decide if that action is a legitimate exercise of an enumerated power or a reasonable application of an implied one. The boundary between state and federal power is constantly being redrawn along this line.

The legislative branch stands as the primary arena for these debates. It is the place where the diverse interests of the American people collide and where the fundamental questions of power and liberty are contested. Designing a bicameral legislature with different methods of election and varying terms of office, the Founders created a system that is intentionally slow and difficult to navigate. This complexity is a safeguard, so that the laws of the nation reflect not just a temporary majority, but a broad and enduring consensus.

Congress remains the "first branch" because it holds the ultimate power of the people: the power to speak the law. Whether through the direct representation of the House or the state-based stability of the Senate, the legislative branch provides the structural foundation for the entire American experiment. Its powers, both enumerated on parchment and implied by necessity, define the scope of the federal government's reach into the lives of its citizens.

Do you believe the 17th Amendment, by shifting the election of senators from state legislatures to the people, fundamentally weakened the principle of federalism by removing the states' direct voice in the national government?

Chapter 8: Congressional Elections and Representation

The House of Representatives serves as the primary link between the American people and their federal government. While the Senate provides stability and represents the states as political entities, the House operates on the principle of direct, popular accountability. Every two years, the entire membership of the House faces the voters. This constant cycle of elections ensures that the chamber remains a sensitive barometer of the national mood. However, the path from a citizen's vote to a representative's seat is governed by a complex set of rules regarding how we count people, where we draw lines, and how we award victory.

Apportionment and Reapportionment

The Constitution mandates that "Representatives and direct Taxes shall be apportioned among the several States... according to their respective Numbers." To achieve this, the government must conduct a census every ten years. This decennial count is the most significant administrative undertaking of the federal government during peacetime. It doesn't just count heads for the sake of data; it determines the distribution of political power and hundreds of billions of dollars in federal funding.

Apportionment is the process of dividing the 435 seats in the House of Representatives among the fifty states based on the census results. While the Constitution originally allowed the House to grow as the population increased, Congress effectively ended this expansion with the **Permanent Apportionment Act of 1929**. This law capped the House at 435 members. Consequently, apportionment has become a "zero-sum game." If one state grows fast enough to gain a seat, another state must lose one.

After the Census Bureau completes the count, it uses a mathematical formula known as the **Method of Equal Proportions** to distribute the seats. This formula aims to minimize the percentage difference in district sizes between states. Every state is constitutionally guaranteed at least one representative, regardless of its population. Currently, states like Wyoming and Vermont have only one representative, while California has over fifty.

Reapportionment refers to the actual reallocation of these seats following the census. This process triggers massive political shifts across the country. In recent decades, the trend has favored the "Sun Belt" states in the South and West at the expense of the "Rust Belt" states in the Northeast and Midwest. For example, states like Texas and Florida have consistently gained seats, reflecting a migration of both people and economic influence. Conversely, states like New York, Pennsylvania, and Ohio have seen their delegations shrink. These shifts don't just affect the House; they also change the balance of the Electoral College, as a state's electoral votes equal its total number of representatives and senators.

The stakes of the census are incredibly high. A minor undercount in a specific city or demographic group can result in a state losing a seat it otherwise would have kept. This leads to intense legal and political battles over census methodology, such as whether to include questions about citizenship or how to handle "hard-to-count" populations in urban and rural areas. Because the census occurs only once a decade, the winners of the reapportionment battle hold their power for ten years, making the process a cornerstone of long-term political strategy.

Redistricting and Gerrymandering

Once the federal government tells a state how many seats it has, the state must decide where the boundaries for those seats will be. This process is called **redistricting**. In most states, the state legislature draws the new map, which the governor must then sign. This gives the political party in power at the state level the opportunity to shape the federal landscape to its advantage.

The Supreme Court has established several ground rules for redistricting. In the 1960s, a series of cases known as the "Reapportionment Revolution" fundamentally changed how districts are drawn. In **Reynolds v. Sims** (1964) and **Wesberry v. Sanders** (1964), the Court established the principle of **"one person, one vote."** This requires that congressional districts within a state be as equal in population as possible. Before these rulings, many states had "silent gerrymanders," where rural districts with few people had the same representation as booming cities. These rulings forced states to draw districts that gave every citizen's vote roughly equal weight.

Despite the requirement for equal population, the *shape* of the districts is often anything but fair. **Gerrymandering** is the practice of drawing district lines to favor a particular party, group, or incumbent. The term originated in 1812 when Massachusetts Governor Elbridge Gerry signed a bill creating a district that critics said looked like a salamander. While the goal has remained the same for two centuries, the methods have become highly sophisticated through the use of big data and advanced mapping software.

Partisan gerrymandering relies on two primary techniques: **packing** and **cracking**.

- **Packing** involves concentrating as many voters of the opposition party as possible into a single district. This allows the opposition to win that one seat by a massive margin but "wastes" their votes, preventing them from influencing neighboring districts.
- **Cracking** involves splitting the opposition party's supporters across multiple districts. By diluting their strength, the party in power ensures that the opposition never reaches a majority in any of those districts.

Technique	Method	Goal
Packing	Concentrating opposition into one district	Wasting opposition votes

Cracking	Spreading opposition across many districts	Preventing an opposition majority

The result of a successful gerrymander is a map where a party can win a majority of a state's house seats even if they lose the statewide popular vote. This creates "safe seats" where the outcome of the general election is a foregone conclusion. In such districts, the only meaningful competition happens in the primary election, which often pushes candidates to more extreme ideological positions to appeal to the party's base.

The Supreme Court's stance on partisan gerrymandering has been a subject of intense debate. In **Rucho v. Common Cause** (2019), the Court ruled that while partisan gerrymandering may be "unjust," it is a "political question" that federal courts cannot resolve. This shifted the battle to state courts and independent commissions. Several states, such as California and Michigan, have moved redistricting authority away from politicians and toward independent, non-partisan commissions to reduce bias.

Racial gerrymandering is a separate legal issue. The **Voting Rights Act of 1965** prohibits states from drawing lines that dilute the voting power of racial minorities.

In some cases, the law actually encourages the creation of "majority-minority" districts to ensure that historically marginalized groups have a fair chance to elect a representative of their choice. However, the Supreme Court ruled in **Shaw v. Reno** (1993) that districts cannot be drawn *solely* on the basis of race without a compelling reason, as this can violate the Equal Protection Clause.

Single-Member Districts

The United States uses a system of **single-member districts** for House elections. This means that each geographic area elects exactly one representative. This system is not a constitutional requirement; for much of the nineteenth century, some states used "at-large" elections where all voters in the state voted for the entire slate of representatives. Congress passed the **Apportionment Act of 1842** to mandate single-member districts, primarily to prevent a single party from sweeping an entire state's delegation.

This system is often paired with **plurality voting**, or "First Past the Post." In this arrangement, the candidate who receives the most votes wins the seat, even if they do not receive an absolute majority (over 50 percent). This is a stark contrast to many European democracies that use **proportional representation**, where parties gain seats based on their percentage of the total national or regional vote.

The use of single-member districts has profound effects on American politics. It encourages a close relationship between the representative and their specific geographic constituency. A representative is expected to be a champion for their district's local economy, infrastructure, and specific needs. This "delegate" model of representation makes House members highly sensitive to local issues, sometimes at the expense of national priorities.

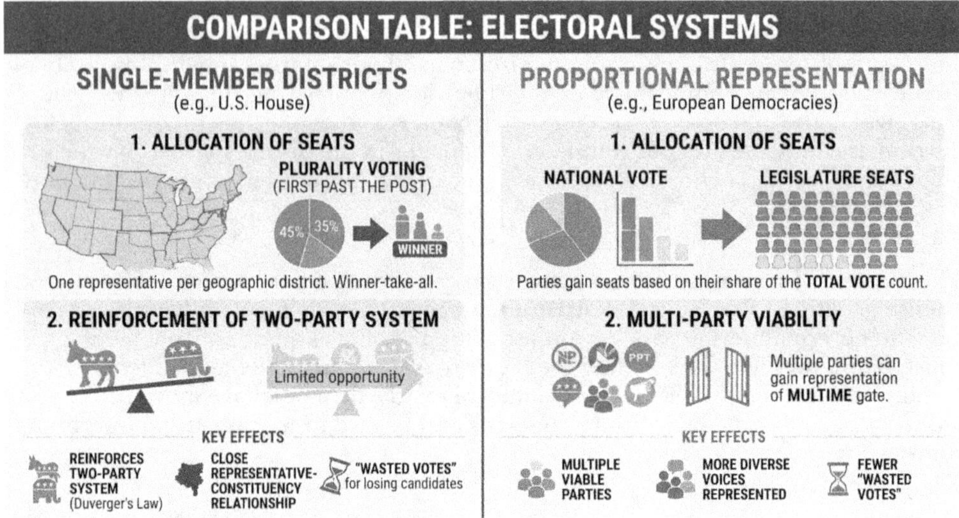

Perhaps the most significant consequence of the single-member district system is the reinforcement of the **two-party system**. This phenomenon is known in political science as **Duverger's Law**. In a winner-take-all district, there is no prize for finishing second or third. This discourages voters from supporting third-party candidates, as they fear "wasting" their vote on someone who cannot win. It also forces diverse political interests to form broad coalitions within the two major parties before the election, rather than forming small, specialized parties that negotiate after the election.

Single-member districts also contribute to the "wasted vote" problem. If a candidate wins a district with 51 percent of the vote, the 49 percent of people who voted for the loser have no representation from their specific choice. In a proportional system, that 49 percent would still contribute to their party's seat count in the legislature. In the American system, the winner represents the entire district, regardless of how thin the margin of victory was.

Incumbency Advantage

One of the most striking features of congressional elections is the **incumbency advantage**. In a typical election cycle, over 90 percent of House members who seek reelection win their seats. Despite low public approval ratings for Congress as an institution, voters tend to like their *own* representative. This phenomenon suggests that once a person gets into office, they possess a formidable set of tools that make it very difficult to unseat them.

The advantage begins with **name recognition**. Most voters cannot name their representative, but they recognize the name on the ballot when they see it. Incumbents spend years building a brand through local news coverage, town hall meetings, and community events. They are the "face" of federal authority in their district.

Incumbents also enjoy significant institutional perks. The **franking privilege** allows members of Congress to send mail to their constituents free of charge. While there are rules against using this for overt campaigning, it allows incumbents to send "newsletters" and "official updates" that keep their name in front of voters at the taxpayers' expense. Furthermore, every representative has a staff dedicated to **casework**. This involves helping constituents navigate the federal bureaucracy – finding a lost Social Security check, helping a veteran get benefits, or assisting with a passport application. When a representative's office solves a problem for a citizen, that citizen (and their family) becomes a loyal voter for life.

Pork barrel spending (or "earmarks") is another key tactic. Representatives work to bring federal projects and money to their specific district. A new bridge, a research grant for a local university, or a contract for a local factory all serve as "proof" that the incumbent is delivering for the district. Voters are often willing to overlook a representative's partisan baggage if they believe the representative is looking out for the local economy.

The most daunting barrier for challengers is **fundraising**. Interest groups and Political Action Committees (PACs) prefer to donate to incumbents because they are a safe bet. No one wants to alienate a sitting committee chair by funding their opponent. As a result, incumbents often enter a race with millions of dollars already in the bank, while challengers must struggle to introduce themselves to the public.

The sheer cost of running a modern campaign, dominated by television advertising and digital outreach, makes the incumbent's financial head start almost insurmountable in many districts.

Factor	Description	Benefit to Incumbent
Casework	Helping constituents with federal agencies	Builds personal loyalty and "non-partisan" support
Franking	Free mail to constituents	Constant, free communication and brand building
Fundraising	Ability to raise large sums from PACs	Outspends challengers; discourages competition
Earmarks	Bringing federal money to the district	Tangible proof of effectiveness for the local area

Finally, the redistricting process itself often protects incumbents. When state legislatures draw maps, they frequently engage in "bipartisan gerrymandering" or "incumbent protection plans." The parties agree to draw districts that are "safe" for the sitting members of both parties, ensuring that neither side faces a serious challenge. This reduces the number of "competitive" districts to a handful nationwide, further solidifying the status quo.

The Problem of Representation

The combination of reapportionment shifts, gerrymandered lines, single-member districts, and the incumbency advantage creates a House of Representatives that is often stable but potentially unresponsive to major shifts in national opinion. When 90 percent of seats are "safe" for one party or the other, the real battle for the soul of the country happens in the primary elections. This shifts power away from the general electorate and toward the most ideological and active members of each party.

This structure also explains why Congress often seems polarized even when the American public is not. Representatives from heavily "packed" or "cracked" districts have no incentive to appeal to the political center. Their only fear is a challenge from their own "flank" in a primary. This leads to a legislature where compromise is viewed as a sign of weakness rather than a necessary part of governance.

The tension at the heart of the House is the desire for local, responsive representation versus the need for a national legislature that can address the country's collective problems. The rules of elections, designed to connect the people to the government, have, in many ways, become a barrier to the very competition they were intended to foster. As the nation moves toward another census and another round of redistricting, the debate over how we choose our leaders remains a fundamental question of American democracy.

While the House was intended to be the "People's House," the administrative and political layers between the voter and the representative have created a system where the lines on a map can be just as important as the names on a ballot. This reality forces us to ask: does the House still represent the people, or does it represent the mapmakers?

> **In your view, would the introduction of multi-member districts with proportional representation be a more effective way to reduce the impact of gerrymandering than the current reliance on independent redistricting commissions?**

Chapter 9: How Congress Organizes Itself

Congress is more than a collection of 535 individual politicians; it is a massive, complex institution that must process thousands of bills, oversee a multi-trillion-dollar budget, and monitor dozens of executive agencies. Without a sophisticated internal structure, the legislative branch would collapse into a state of permanent stalemate. To manage this workload, Congress organizes itself through two primary mechanisms: a partisan leadership hierarchy and a specialized committee system.

While the Constitution provides the broad outlines of the House and Senate, it says remarkably little about how these bodies should actually function day to day. It mentions the Speaker of the House and the Vice President's role in the Senate, but the vast network of floor leaders, whips, and committee chairs emerged over two centuries of trial, error, and political necessity. This organization isn't just about efficiency, but about power. Whoever controls the schedule and the committees controls the national agenda.

Party Leadership in the House

The House of Representatives is a majoritarian institution where the majority party wields nearly total control over the legislative process. Because the House is so large, it requires a rigid, hierarchical structure to function.

At the top of this pyramid sits the **Speaker of the House**, the most powerful individual in Congress. The Speaker is the only House officer mentioned in the Constitution and stands second in the line of presidential succession, immediately following the Vice President.

The majority party chooses the Speaker, which gives the office a dual identity. The Speaker is both the presiding officer of the entire House and the leader of their political party. They exercise power by appointing members to the influential **Rules Committee**, referring bills to specific committees, and controlling which pieces of legislation actually reach the floor for a vote.

If the Speaker doesn't want a bill to pass, it typically never sees the light of day. This "gatekeeping" authority makes the Speaker the primary architect of the House's legislative strategy.

Assisting the Speaker is the **House Majority Leader**. While the Speaker focuses on the big-picture strategy and constitutional duties, the Majority Leader manages the daily legislative schedule. They work with committee chairs to ensure that bills are ready for floor debate and serve as the party's primary spokesperson during floor proceedings. Below the Majority Leader is the **Majority Whip**. The term "whip" comes from the "whipper-in" in British fox hunting, who keeps the hounds from straying. In Congress, the whip's job is to count votes before they happen and ensure that party members show up to vote in alignment with the leadership's wishes.

The minority party organizes itself in a similar fashion, led by the **House Minority Leader** and the **Minority Whip**. Because the House rules favor the majority so heavily, the Minority Leader's primary goal is usually to maintain party unity and offer an alternative vision to the public. They have little power to move their own legislation, so they focus on criticizing the majority and preparing for the next election.

One of the most effective tools of House leadership is the **House Rules Committee**. Often called the "Traffic Cop" of the House, this committee determines the "rules" for every bill that reaches the floor. These rules specify how much time is allowed for debate and whether any amendments can be offered. By issuing a "closed rule," the leadership can prevent the minority party from proposing changes to a bill, forcing a simple up-or-down vote. This level of control is unique to the House and ensures that the majority party can deliver on its policy promises.

Party Leadership in the Senate

The Senate is a far more individualistic and less hierarchical body than the House. Its rules protect the rights of the minority and even individual senators. Consequently, leadership in the Senate is more about persuasion and negotiation than command and control.

The Constitution names the Vice President as the **President of the Senate**, but this is largely a ceremonial role. The Vice President rarely appears in the chamber except to break a tie or preside over major events.

In the Vice President's absence, the **President Pro Tempore** presides. This position usually goes to the most senior member of the majority party. Like the Vice President's role, this is mostly a title of honor with little actual power. The real authority in the Senate rests with the **Senate Majority Leader**.

The Senate Majority Leader is the equivalent of the House Speaker in terms of political influence, but they lack the same formal powers. They cannot simply decree that a bill will be debated. Instead, they must often rely on **unanimous consent agreements** to manage the Senate's schedule. If a single senator objects to the schedule, the Majority Leader must find a way to compromise or resort to more complex procedural maneuvers. This makes the Senate Majority Leader a "first among equals" rather than a supreme commander.

The Senate Minority Leader holds significantly more leverage than their House counterpart. Because the Senate rules allow for the **filibuster** (prolonged speech intended to delay or block a vote), the minority party can stop almost any legislation that doesn't have the support of sixty senators. This means the Majority and Minority Leaders must constantly communicate. Most major Senate business is conducted through a delicate dance of bipartisan negotiation, as the Majority Leader knows that a disgruntled minority can bring the entire chamber to a halt.

(This photo captures Senator Huey Long of Louisiana at the height of his theatrical style, arms raised triumphantly after a marathon filibuster. Rather than quiet obstruction, Long turned the tactic into political performance. He used extended floor speeches to draw public attention, pressure opponents, and position himself as a populist fighting entrenched power.)

Whips exist in the Senate just as they do in the House, but their job is often more difficult. Senators represent entire states and have six-year terms, making them more independent than House members. A senator may be more worried about their state's specific industry or their personal ideology than the party's national platform. Senate whips must be masters of personal relationships, often trading favors or committee assignments to secure a single, vital vote.

The Committee System

While the floor leaders handle the politics and the schedule, the actual work of lawmaking happens in the **committee system**. Woodrow Wilson, before becoming president, famously observed that "Congress in session is Congress on public exhibition, whilst Congress in its committee-rooms is Congress at work." Committees are the "engine rooms" of the legislative branch, where bills are drafted, debated, and refined before they ever reach the full House or Senate.

The primary rationale for committees is **specialization**. It is impossible for any single representative or senator to be an expert on everything from nuclear energy to wheat subsidies to international trade. By dividing into committees, members of

Congress can develop deep expertise in specific policy areas. This allows for more informed legislating and more effective oversight of the executive branch.

When a bill is introduced, it is referred to a committee with jurisdiction over that subject. The committee chair, always a member of the majority party, then decides the bill's fate. They can choose to hold hearings, where experts and interest groups testify, or they can simply "pigeonhole" the bill, letting it die without any action. Most bills introduced in Congress die in committee.

If a committee decides to move forward, it holds a **markup session**. During markup, committee members go through the bill line by line, proposing amendments and rewriting sections. This is where the real compromises are made. Once a bill is "reported out" of committee, it goes to the full chamber for consideration. The members of the committee then act as "floor managers," explaining the bill to their colleagues and defending it during debate.

Committee chairs are among the most powerful figures in Washington. They control the committee's budget, set its agenda, and lead the staff. For decades, chairs were chosen strictly by the **seniority system**, which meant the member of the majority party who had served the longest on the committee got the job.

Today, party leadership and the party caucus have more say in who becomes a chair, though seniority still remains a major factor. This shift has made chairs more accountable to their party's national goals.

Types of Committees

Congress utilizes four different types of committees, each serving a distinct function in the legislative or oversight process.

Standing committees are the most important and the only ones with the power to propose legislation. They are permanent bodies that continue from one Congress to the next. Examples include the House Ways and Means Committee (which handles taxes) and the Senate Foreign Relations Committee.

Most standing committees are further divided into **subcommittees**, which focus on even more specific issues, such as the Subcommittee on Livestock and Foreign Agriculture.

Select committees (or special committees) are usually temporary and created for a specific purpose. They often conduct investigations rather than draft legislation. For example, Congress might create a select committee to investigate a specific scandal, a natural disaster response, or a new emerging threat like cyberwarfare. While they usually disappear once their task is complete, some, like the House Permanent Select Committee on Intelligence, eventually become permanent.

Joint committees consist of members from both the House and the Senate. They are primarily focused on administrative matters or long-term economic studies. They do not have the authority to report legislation to the floor. The Joint Committee on the Library and the Joint Committee on Taxation are examples of these bodies. They serve to coordinate efforts between the two chambers on non-legislative issues.

Conference committees are a special type of joint committee created for a very specific, short-term goal: resolving differences between House and Senate versions of the same bill.

For a bill to become law, it must pass both chambers in identical form. If the House and Senate pass different versions, a conference committee (composed of members from the original standing committees that handled the bill) meets to hammer out a compromise. Once they reach an agreement, the "conference report" goes back to both chambers for a final, up-or-down vote.

Committee Type	Permanent or Temporary?	Proposes Legislation?	Composition
Standing	Permanent	Yes	One chamber only
Select	Usually Temporary	No (usually)	One chamber only
Joint	Permanent	No	Both chambers
Conference	Temporary	No (reconciles only)	Both chambers

Caucuses and Conferences

Beyond the formal leadership and committee structures, Congress is organized into informal groups known as **caucuses** (or "conferences" in some contexts). These groups are voluntary associations of members who share a common interest, identity, or geographic background. They allow members to coordinate strategy, share information, and advocate for specific issues outside the official party and committee lines.

The most fundamental caucuses are the **party caucuses** (the House Democratic Caucus and the House Republican Conference). These groups meet behind closed doors to elect their leaders, approve committee assignments, and hammer out the party's official position on major bills. These meetings are where the internal party "family fights" happen before a united front is presented to the public.

There are also hundreds of **special interest caucuses**. Some are based on regional concerns, like the Great Lakes Task Force or the Rural Caucus. Others are based on identity, such as the Congressional Black Caucus, the Congressional Hispanic Caucus, or the Congressional Caucus for Women's Issues. These groups are incredibly influential because they can mobilize a block of votes across different committees. If the Congressional Black Caucus decides to oppose a bill, the Democratic leadership must take that opposition seriously to maintain its coalition.

Some caucuses are purely ideological. The House Freedom Caucus, for example, consists of conservative Republicans who often push their party leadership to the right. The Progressive Caucus does the same for the Democrats on the left. These groups often act as "parties within parties," creating their own legislative agendas and sometimes even challenging their own party leaders on the floor.

Caucuses provide a way for members to build relationships and gain influence outside the rigid seniority system of the committees. A junior member might not have much power on the Appropriations Committee, but they could be a leader in the Climate Solutions Caucus.

This informal network adds another layer of complexity to the legislative process, as leaders must negotiate not just with individuals or committee chairs, but with these organized blocs of members.

Staff and Support Agencies

Congress does not work alone. The institution is supported by thousands of professional staffers and several non-partisan support agencies. Each member has a personal staff to handle constituent services, communications, and policy research. Committees have their own professional staffs, often consisting of lawyers and subject-matter experts who do the heavy lifting of drafting bill text and organizing hearings.

Three key agencies provide Congress with the independent data it needs to check the executive branch.

The **Congressional Budget Office (CBO)** provides non-partisan economic analyses and "scores" bills to determine their long-term cost.

The **Government Accountability Office (GAO)** acts as the "watchdog" for Congress, auditing executive agencies to ensure they are spending money legally and efficiently.

The **Congressional Research Service (CRS)** functions as a private library and think tank for members, providing neutral, expert reports on any policy topic imaginable.

These agencies are essential for the separation of powers. Without them, Congress would have to rely on the executive branch for information, which would make it impossible to provide effective oversight. By having its own sources of data and expertise, Congress maintains its intellectual independence.

The Dynamics of Power

The organization of Congress is a study in the balance between individual freedom and collective action. In the House, the system favors collective action through strong party leadership. In the Senate, the system protects individual freedom through its deliberative rules. In both chambers, the committee system decentralizes power, giving small groups of members immense influence over specific parts of American life.

This organization creates a "fragmented" legislative process. Because a bill must pass through subcommittees, committees, the Rules Committee (in the House), floor leaders, and potentially a conference committee, there are dozens of "veto points" where a bill can be killed.

This is exactly what the Founders intended. They wanted a system where it was difficult to pass laws, ensuring that only those with broad and sustained support could survive the gauntlet.

The partisan nature of this organization has intensified in recent years. As the parties have become more ideologically distinct, the power of party leaders has grown. Speakers and Majority Leaders now use their control over the schedule and committee assignments to enforce party discipline more strictly than in the past. This has led to a more "top-down" legislative process, where major deals are often negotiated by a few top leaders behind closed doors and then presented to the rank-and-file members for a vote.

Despite these changes, the fundamental structure remains. Congress is still a body of representatives who must answer to their constituents, organized into a system that rewards expertise and seniority. The tension between the formal rules of the committees and the informal power of the caucuses, and between the hierarchical House and the individualistic Senate, is what makes the United States Congress the most complex and powerful legislature in the world.

Understanding how Congress organizes itself is essential for understanding why certain laws pass and others fail. It isn't just about who has the most votes; it's about who controls the process. The "how" of Congress is just as important as the "who."

Does the modern trend toward "top-down" leadership, where major bills are negotiated by a few leaders rather than through the traditional committee process, undermine the benefits of specialization that the committee system was designed to provide?

Chapter 10: The Legislative Process

The path a bill travels from a mere idea to the United States Code is designed to be an arduous obstacle course. It isn't a factory assembly line where raw materials predictably emerge as finished products. Instead, it is a gauntlet of "veto points" where a single determined opponent or a procedural misstep can kill a proposal instantly. The Framers intended this friction. They wanted to ensure that the national government could only act when a broad, sustained consensus existed across different branches and constituencies. To understand the legislative process is to understand why most ideas in Washington fail and why the few that survive carry such immense weight.

Bill Introduction and Sponsorship

Every piece of federal legislation begins with a **sponsor**. While ideas for laws come from the President, interest groups, or concerned citizens, only a member of Congress has the legal authority to formally introduce a bill.

In the House of Representatives, this is a relatively quiet affair. A member simply places the draft in a wooden box known as the **hopper** on the side of the Clerk's desk. In the Senate, the process is slightly more formal; a senator usually introduces a bill from the floor, often accompanied by a speech explaining its necessity.

Bills are designated as "H.R." in the House or "S." in the Senate, followed by a number assigned in the order of introduction. A bill can have **cosponsors**, other members who add their names to the legislation to show broad support. "Primary" cosponsors are usually the ones who helped draft the bill, while others might join later to signal their party's commitment to the cause. Having a large, bipartisan list of cosponsors doesn't guarantee a bill's success, but it serves as a vital signal to the leadership that the proposal has legs.

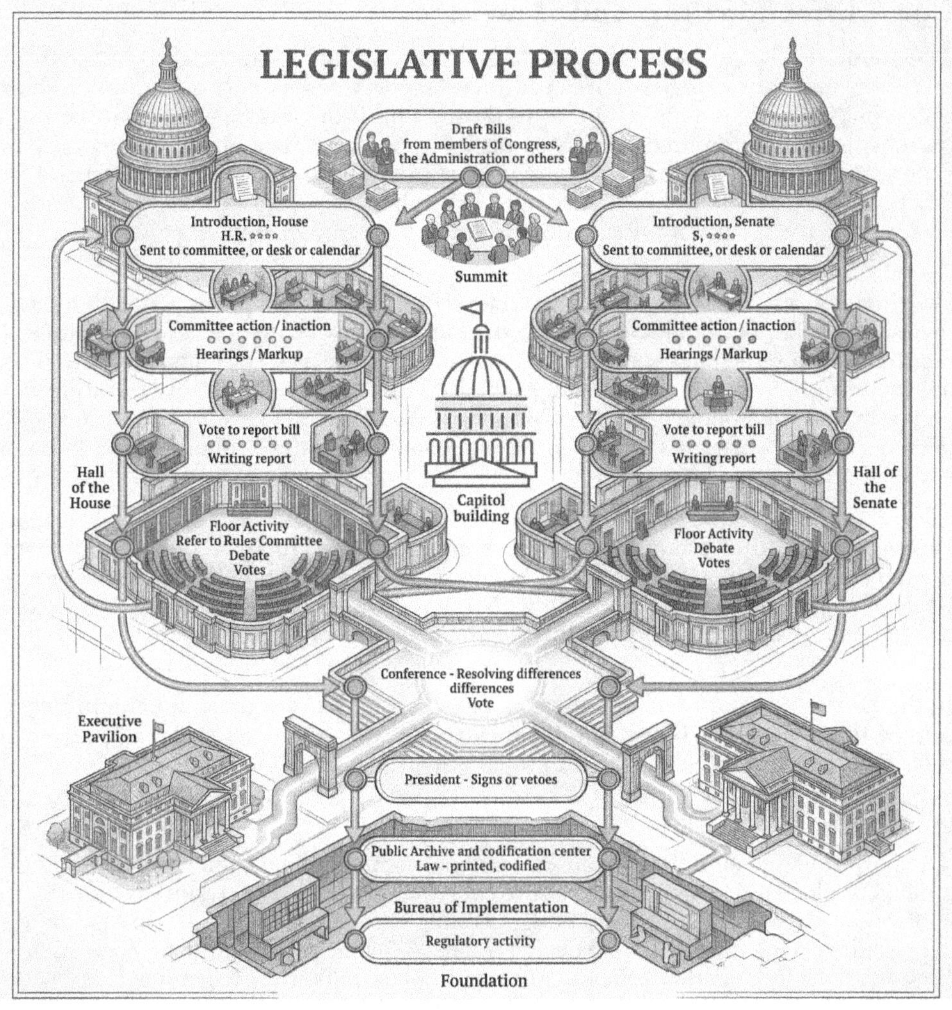

Legislation generally falls into two categories: public bills and private bills. Public bills deal with matters of general importance and apply to the entire nation, such as tax changes or environmental regulations. Private bills are rarer and apply to specific individuals or places, often dealing with immigration status or personal claims against the government. Congress also uses various types of **resolutions**. Simple and concurrent resolutions don't have the force of law and don't require the President's signature; they are used for internal rules or to express the "sense of Congress" on an issue. Joint resolutions, however, are essentially the same as bills and carry the full weight of law if passed and signed.

Once a bill is introduced, it is "read" into the record and referred to a committee. This referral is a critical moment of gatekeeping. The Parliamentarian of each chamber decides which committee has jurisdiction over the bill's subject matter. If a bill is poorly drafted or covers too many topics, it might be sent to multiple committees (multiple referral), which significantly decreases its chances of survival because it must now please twice as many critics.

Committee Markup and Hearings

The committee stage is where most bills go to die. Statistics show that roughly 90 percent of introduced legislation never makes it past this phase. If a committee chair likes a bill, they will schedule it for a **hearing**. This is the investigative phase of lawmaking. The committee invites "witnesses" (government officials, industry experts, academics, or activists) to provide testimony. These hearings serve several functions: they build a public record, allow members to "posture" for the cameras, and provide the technical information necessary to refine the bill's language.

Hearings are often the only time the public sees the legislative process in action, but the real work happens afterward in the **markup** session. This is where committee members debate the bill's specific language and propose amendments. It's a grueling, line-by-line process. Members might argue for hours over a single word or a specific dollar amount in a budget. If the committee is deeply divided, the markup can become a theater of partisan combat. If the committee is functional, the markup is a masterclass in compromise.

During markup, the committee has several options. It can report the bill favorably to the full chamber, report it with amendments, or draft a "clean bill" that incorporates all the changes into a new document with a new number. If a committee refuses to act on a bill, it is effectively dead (this is known as "pigeonholing").

In the House, a majority of members can force a bill out of a reluctant committee using a **discharge petition**, but this is extremely difficult to achieve and rarely succeeds. It requires 218 signatures, which means members must defy their own party leadership.

The power of the committee chair cannot be overstated. The chair decides whether a bill gets a hearing, which witnesses are called, and when the markup occurs. They control the committee's staff and budget. While modern party rules have slightly clipped their wings, a committee chair remains a formidable baron who can stall a President's entire agenda by simply refusing to put a bill on the calendar.

Scheduling for the Floor

If a bill survives the committee, it is "placed on the calendar." However, being on the calendar doesn't mean the bill will ever be debated. In the House, the **Rules Committee** acts as a second gatekeeper. It is often called the "arm of the leadership" because the Speaker appoints most of its members. The Rules Committee issues a "rule" for each bill, which dictates how much time is allowed for debate and what kind of amendments are permitted.

- **Open Rule -** Allows any member to propose any amendment that is germane (relevant) to the bill.
- **Closed Rule -** Prohibits all amendments, forcing a simple up-or-down vote. This is common for complex tax or trade bills.
- **Modified Rule -** Allows only specific amendments that have been pre-approved by the committee.

In the Senate, scheduling is much looser and relies on **unanimous consent agreements**. Because any single senator can object to the schedule, the Majority Leader must negotiate with the Minority Leader and often with individual senators to set the terms of debate. If a senator believes a bill will harm their state, they may place a "hold" on it, signaling that they will object to any unanimous consent request. While a hold isn't a formal rule, it serves as a warning that a filibuster is coming.

Floor Debate and Amendment

Floor debate is the most visible part of the process, but the two chambers handle it very differently. In the House, debate is strictly limited. The "Committee of the Whole" (a parliamentary device that allows the House to function with fewer members present) usually handles the amending process. Members are often limited to five minutes of speaking time. All amendments must be **germane**, meaning they must relate directly to the topic of the bill. This prevents members from "hitching a ride" on a popular bill by adding unrelated provisions.

The Senate, by contrast, is a body defined by unlimited debate. There is no requirement that amendments be germane, except in very specific circumstances. This allows senators to add **riders** (provisions that have nothing to do with the main bill) to any piece of legislation moving through the chamber. This is why a bill about highway funding might suddenly include an amendment about offshore drilling or student loans.

Voting on the floor takes several forms. A **voice vote** ("Aye" or "No") is common for non-controversial items. If the result is unclear, a member can call for a **division vote**, where members stand to be counted. The most important votes are **recorded votes** (or roll-call votes), where each member's choice is documented.

In the House, this is done electronically; in the Senate, the clerk calls each name aloud. These records are vital for accountability, as they allow constituents to see exactly where their representative stands.

The Filibuster and Cloture

The **filibuster** is the most distinctive and controversial feature of the Senate. It is the practice of using long speeches or procedural delays to prevent a vote on a bill. Because the Senate has no general rule limiting debate, a senator can keep talking indefinitely, provided they stay on the floor and continue speaking. The goal is to "talk the bill to death" or force the majority to withdraw it.

Modern filibusters rarely involve a senator actually speaking for twenty-four hours straight (the "talking filibuster"). Instead, we have the "silent filibuster." A senator simply informs the leadership that they intend to filibuster, and unless the majority can find sixty votes to stop them, the bill is pulled from the floor. This has effectively turned the Senate into a "super-majority" institution where almost all major legislation requires 60 votes to pass, rather than a simple majority of 51.

The only way to stop a filibuster is through **cloture**. This process is governed by **Rule 22**. It requires a petition signed by sixteen senators and a vote of three-fifths of the full Senate (usually 60 votes). If cloture is invoked, debate is limited to an additional thirty hours, after which a final vote must be taken.

Feature	The House of Representatives	The Senate
Debate Time	Strictly limited by the Rules Committee	Generally unlimited
Amendments	Must be germane	Can be unrelated (riders)
Process Speed	Can move very fast with a majority	Slow, deliberate, and easily blocked
Obstruction	Hard for individuals to block action	Easy for a single senator to delay

The filibuster is often defended as a tool for protecting the minority from the "tyranny of the majority." It forces the two parties to compromise and ensures that massive changes to American law have broad support. Critics, however, argue that it leads to permanent gridlock and allows a small minority of the population (represented by senators from small states) to block the will of the national majority. In recent years, both parties have used the "nuclear option" (a procedural maneuver that changes Senate rules by a simple majority) to eliminate the filibuster for judicial and executive branch appointments. However, it still remains in place for most general legislation.

Conference Committees

The Constitution mandates that the House of Representatives and the Senate must agree on the exact same sequence of words before a bill moves to the president's desk. This requirement sounds simple in theory, but it becomes a logistical nightmare when two different bodies, representing different constituencies and operating under different rules, take turns rewriting a proposal. Legislation rarely survives this journey without being nipped and tucked in ways that please one side but alienate the other.

If the House passes a bill to spend fifty million dollars on rural broadband and the Senate changes that number to forty million, the two versions are legally distinct. They cannot both go to the White House. This necessity for absolute textual symmetry creates the need for the **conference committee**.

Political scientists often call the conference committee the "third house of Congress." It is a temporary, ad hoc entity created for the sole purpose of resolving the differences between two versions of a single bill. It possesses no permanent staff and no standing jurisdiction. It exists only until it produces a compromise or until its members admit they cannot find common ground. Because it holds the power to decide the final form of major laws, it is arguably one of the most significant points of influence in the entire federal government. It is the place where the broad outlines of a policy are turned into the specific, enforceable details that govern the nation.

The members of this group are known as **conferees**. Convention dictates that they are drawn from the standing committees that originally reviewed and reported the bill. In practice, this means the most senior members and the committee chairs from both parties and both chambers sit across from each other. The Speaker of the House and the Senate Majority Leader choose these representatives, often using the appointments as a reward for party loyalty or as a way to ensure their specific policy goals remain in the final text. This ensures that the people who know the technical details of the bill are the ones negotiating its final shape. Usually, the number of conferees from each chamber doesn't have to be equal because each side votes as a unit. For a compromise to move forward, a majority of the House conferees and a majority of the Senate conferees must sign off on the deal.

These negotiators operate under strict, though sometimes flexible, rules. They are technically forbidden from adding completely new material that wasn't included in either the House or the Senate version. If the House passed a bill on tax credits and the Senate passed a bill on tax credits, the conferees cannot suddenly add a section about national parks. This is known as staying within the "scope of the differences." If they ignore this rule, any member of either chamber can raise a "point of order" to block the bill.

Within that scope, however, they have immense latitude. If one chamber wants a five percent tax and the other wants ten percent, the conference committee can land anywhere between those two numbers. They spend hours, sometimes days, horse-trading over these specific discrepancies. One side might agree to a lower funding level for a specific project if the other side agrees to a stricter enforcement deadline for a different regulation. This is the essence of legislative compromise. It is a zero-sum game played with the nation's budget and legal code.

When a majority of the conferees from each chamber agree on a compromise, they produce a **conference report**. This document contains the final, negotiated text of the bill along with a joint explanatory statement that outlines the changes. The report then travels back to the House and the Senate for a final vote.

At this stage, the rules are unforgiving. No member can propose further amendments or changes. The chambers must vote on the report as a whole (a take-it-or-leave-it proposition). This all-or-nothing vote prevents the bill from falling back into the cycle of endless amendments that required the conference in the first place. If both chambers approve the report, the bill is "enrolled" and sent to the White House for the president's signature.

In some cases, the differences between the two chambers are minor enough that a formal conference isn't necessary. This process is called "concurring in the amendment." If the Senate makes a few small changes to a House bill and the House agrees to them, the process ends there. This is a common way to handle non-controversial legislation or bills that need to move quickly during an emergency. It avoids the administrative burden of setting up a formal committee and appointing negotiators.

The formal conference committee has become an endangered species in the twenty-first century. For decades, it was the standard way of doing business, but today's party leaders increasingly view it as a liability. A formal conference is relatively public, it involves a wide range of members, and it gives disgruntled committee chairs a chance to block the party's national agenda. In a highly polarized environment, leaders want to minimize the number of people who have a say in the final deal. To avoid these risks, leadership teams now prefer a process colloquially known as **ping-ponging**.

In a ping-pong scenario, the House sends an amendment to the Senate, and the Senate sends its own version back to the House. This back-and-forth continues until both sides agree on the text. This method keeps the decision-making power in the hands of a few top leaders and their hand-picked staffers. It bypasses the rank-and-file committee members and ensures that the final deal is hammered out behind closed doors in the Speaker's or the Majority Leader's office. This shift reflects the broader centralization of power in Congress, where the traditional, decentralized committee process is sacrificed for partisan efficiency.

When a bill skips the formal conference, the public loses the ability to see who is trading what and why. It consolidates the final word on national policy into the hands of a very small group of people. While this makes the process faster, it also makes it less transparent and arguably less representative. The decline of the conference committee signals a fundamental change in how the United States makes its laws. It has moved from a deliberative process involving experts and committee members to a strategic game played by the highest levels of party leadership.

Despite its decline, the concept of the conference committee remains a vital part of the constitutional architecture. It represents the final moment of reconciliation in a system designed to be divided. It is the mechanism that forces the House and the Senate to stop acting like rivals and start acting like a single legislature. Whether it happens in a formal room with conferees or through the electronic ping-ponging of amendments, the goal remains the same: the creation of a single, unified law that carries the consent of both chambers of the people's representatives. Without this moment of textual agreement, the entire legislative engine would grind to a halt.

Presidential Signature and Veto

The final step in the process belongs to the President. Once a bill reaches the Oval Office, the President has ten days (not counting Sundays) to act. The President has four options:

1. **Sign the bill -** The bill becomes law immediately.
2. **Veto the bill -** The President sends the bill back to the chamber where it originated with a "veto message" explaining why they disagree with it.
3. **Do nothing (while Congress is in session) -** If the President does nothing for ten days and Congress is still in session, the bill becomes law without a signature. This is a way for a President to express disapproval without taking the political risk of a formal veto.
4. **The Pocket Veto -** If the President does nothing for ten days and Congress adjourns during that time, the bill dies. This is called a "pocket veto" because the President has effectively put the bill in their pocket and walked away. This type

of veto cannot be overridden because Congress is no longer in session to vote on it.

If the President issues a formal veto, Congress can attempt a **veto override**. This is the ultimate check in the system. It requires a **two-thirds majority** vote in both the House and the Senate. Overrides are rare because they require a high level of bipartisan cooperation. Since 1789, only about 100 out of every 1,500 vetoes have been successfully overridden. If an override succeeds, the bill becomes law despite the President's objection.

The veto is a powerful tactic for executive influence. Even the *threat* of a veto can change the entire legislative process. If a President lets it be known that they will veto a bill unless a certain provision is removed, Congress will often comply rather than see months of work go to waste. This "veto bargaining" makes the President a silent partner in almost every major legislative negotiation.

The Complexity of the Process

The legislative process is not a linear path but a series of interlocking circles. A bill can be sent back to committee at almost any time. It can be amended on the floor, stripped in a conference committee, and vetoed at the finish line. Every step requires a different coalition of supporters. The group of members who support a bill in the House may be very different from the group that supports it in the Senate.

This complexity serves a specific purpose. It protects the status quo. In the American system, it is much easier to stop a law than it is to pass one. This ensures that the laws that *do* pass are usually the result of intense negotiation and broad consensus. While this can be frustrating for those who want quick action on national problems, it also prevents the government from making sudden, radical changes that might destabilize the country.

The process also reflects the reality of **political parties**. While the formal steps of the process are written in the Constitution and the rules of the chambers, the way those steps are executed depends on which party is in power. A "unified government" (where one party controls the House, the Senate, and the Presidency) moves much differently than a "divided government." In times of high polarization, the procedural tools like the filibuster and the Rules Committee become weapons in a larger partisan war.

In the end, the legislative process is the heart of American democracy. It is where the diverse interests of a continental nation are brought together to find a common path. It is messy, slow, and often frustrating, but it is the only way to ensure that the laws of the land carry the "consent of the governed." Each bill that becomes law represents a triumph of cooperation over conflict, a moment where the system's friction was overcome by the necessity of action.

> **Given the frequency of "silent filibusters" and the requirement for 60 votes in the Senate, has the legislative process become so difficult that it now favors stagnation over the "more perfect Union" promised in the Preamble?**

Chapter 11: Congressional Powers Beyond Lawmaking

Congress frequently appears in the public imagination as a legislative factory, a place where bills are debated, amended, and occasionally passed into law. However, the American constitutional design grants the legislature a vast array of authorities that have nothing to do with drafting statutes. These non-legislative powers ensure that the House and Senate function as the primary check on the executive and judicial branches. Without these tools, the legislature would be a passive observer of the President's actions, unable to enforce the will of the people or protect the treasury from waste and abuse.

The Power of the Purse

The most formidable authority in the congressional arsenal is the power of the purse. Article I, Section 9, Clause 7 of the Constitution provides that "No Money shall be drawn from the Treasury, but in Consequence of Appropriations made by Law." This simple sentence creates the ultimate barrier to executive overreach.

The President can command the world's most formidable military and manage millions of federal employees, but he can't pay a single soldier or buy a single paperclip without an explicit act of Congress.

This authority functions through a two-step process: **authorization** and **appropriation**. First, Congress must pass an authorization bill that creates or continues a federal agency or program. This act establishes the legal framework and sets a ceiling on how much money the program might receive. However, an authorization doesn't actually provide the cash. That happens in the second step: the appropriations bill. The Appropriations Committees in the House and Senate decide exactly how much money each authorized program will actually receive for the upcoming fiscal year.

This two-step system gives Congress multiple opportunities to influence executive policy. If the legislature dislikes how a particular department is operating, it can "starve" the agency by cutting its budget or placing specific "riders" on its funding. These riders are provisions that prohibit an agency from spending money on specific activities. For example, Congress has frequently used appropriations bills to prevent the executive branch from moving prisoners out of the Guantanamo Bay detention camp or to block the implementation of specific environmental regulations.

The **Antideficiency Act** further solidifies this power by making it a legal violation for executive officials to spend money that Congress hasn't appropriated or to involve the government in contracts before an appropriation is made. This prevents the executive branch from "forcing" the legislature's hand by creating debts that Congress feels morally or legally obligated to pay.

The debt ceiling represents another facet of this fiscal authority. While Congress authorizes spending, it also sets a legal limit on how much the federal government can borrow to pay for that spending. This creates a recurring political flashpoint.

When the government approaches this limit, the President must ask Congress to raise it. This provides the legislature with a massive lever to demand policy concessions from the White House, even if the spending in question was already authorized in previous years.

Congress also uses the power of the purse to influence state governments. Through **categorical grants** and block grants, the federal government provides funds for education, transportation, and healthcare. However, these funds often come with "strings attached." If a state wants federal highway money, it must comply with federal standards for speed limits or the legal drinking age. This allows Congress to shape policy in areas that the Constitution technically reserves to the states.

Oversight and Investigation

If the power of the purse is the legislature's muscle, oversight and investigation are its eyes and ears. While the Constitution does not explicitly use the word "oversight," the Supreme Court has long recognized it as an implied power essential to the legislative function.

To make good laws, Congress must understand how the current laws are being executed. To spend money wisely, it must know how the current money is being wasted.

Congressional oversight involves the ongoing review, monitoring, and supervision of federal agencies, programs, and policy implementation. Most of this work occurs within the standing committees. These bodies hold regular hearings where cabinet secretaries and agency heads must testify under oath. This public questioning forces executive officials to justify their decisions and account for their failures.

The **Government Accountability Office (GAO)** serves as the primary investigative arm of Congress. Known as the "congressional watchdog," the GAO is a non-partisan agency that audits federal programs and reports on how effectively the executive branch is spending taxpayer dollars. If an agency is mismanaging a project or ignoring a congressional mandate, the GAO finds the evidence and presents it to the relevant committees.

When an agency is uncooperative, Congress can use its **subpoena power**. A subpoena is a legal order requiring an individual to testify or produce documents. If an official refuses to comply, Congress can hold them in **contempt**. This can lead to civil lawsuits or, in rare cases, criminal prosecution. The threat of a subpoena is often enough to compel an agency to release information it would otherwise prefer to keep secret.

Oversight Tool	Function	Source of Authority
Hearings	Public questioning of officials	Implied (Article I)
GAO Audits	Independent financial/policy review	Statutory (GAO Act)
Subpoena	Compels testimony and documents	Implied/Inherent
Casework	Monitoring agency service to citizens	Representational role

Oversight also includes the "sunset" provision, where Congress gives a program an expiration date. To keep the program alive, the executive branch must prove its effectiveness to the legislature. This forces a periodic and thorough review of whether a government function still serves the national interest.

Sometimes oversight turns into a full-scale investigation. This often happens after a major national failure or scandal. The investigations into the 9/11 attacks, the Watergate scandal, and the response to Hurricane Katrina were all led by congressional committees. These investigations aren't just about finding blame; they are about identifying systemic weaknesses and proposing legislative fixes to prevent a recurrence.

Impeachment Authority

The most dramatic non-legislative power is the authority to remove federal officials from office. The Framers included the impeachment process as a "safety valve" to protect the republic from "Treason, Bribery, or other high Crimes and Misdemeanors." This authority applies to the President, Vice President, and all "civil Officers of the United States," which includes federal judges and cabinet members.

Impeachment is a two-stage process that involves both chambers of Congress. The **House of Representatives** holds the sole power to impeach, which is the equivalent of a grand jury indictment. A simple majority vote in the House is sufficient to formally charge an official with a crime or abuse of power. If the House votes to impeach, the official is not yet removed; they have merely been "impeached."

The second stage is the trial, which takes place in the **Senate**. Here, the Senate sits as a jury, and a group of House members, known as "managers," act as prosecutors. If the President is on trial, the Chief Justice of the Supreme Court presides over the proceedings to prevent the Vice President (who is the President of the Senate) from having a conflict of interest.

A conviction requires a **two-thirds majority** of the senators present. This high bar ensures that an official cannot be removed for purely partisan reasons; there must be a broad, bipartisan consensus that the official is unfit for office. If the Senate convicts, the official is immediately removed and may be barred from holding any future federal office. The Senate cannot impose prison time or fines, although the removed official remains subject to criminal prosecution in regular courts.

Impeachment Phase	Body Responsible	Vote Required	Result
Impeachment	House of Representatives	Simple Majority	Formal charges filed
Trial	Senate	N/A	Evidence presented
Conviction	Senate	Two-Thirds	Removal from office

Historically, the impeachment of judges is more common than the impeachment of presidents. Because federal judges serve for life, impeachment is the only way to remove a judge who is corrupt or incompetent.

In the case of presidents, the process is incredibly rare and politically explosive. It represents the ultimate struggle between the legislative and executive branches, a moment when the representatives of the people decide that the head of state has forfeited his mandate.

The phrase "high Crimes and Misdemeanors" remains one of the most debated aspects of this power. It doesn't necessarily refer to violations of the criminal code. Instead, it encompasses political offenses against the state itself, such as a gross breach of public trust or the misuse of official authority for personal gain. Because the Constitution provides no precise definition, each Congress must determine for itself where the line between a political disagreement and an impeachable offense exists.

During the Senate trial, the chamber adopts a quasi-judicial character. Senators take a special oath to provide impartial justice, though their roles as political representatives often conflict with their roles as jurors. The presence of the Chief Justice adds a layer of solemnity and procedural expertise, yet the Senate maintains the final authority to determine the rules of the proceeding. This independence ensures that the judiciary cannot interfere with what is fundamentally a legislative decision.

The Supreme Court confirmed this in *Nixon v. United States* (1993), ruling that the courts cannot review impeachment proceedings because the Constitution gives the Senate the "sole" power to try such cases. This makes the legislature the final judge of its own process.

Disqualification from future office requires a separate, secondary vote that occurs only after a conviction. While the Constitution mandates removal upon conviction, it leaves disqualification to the Senate's discretion. This ensures the "safety valve" not only removes a dangerous official but can also permanently prevent their return to any position of public honor or trust.

Treaty Ratification and Confirmations

The Senate holds two unique powers that the House does not: the authority to approve treaties and the duty to confirm presidential appointments. These functions are known collectively as **Advice and Consent**. They ensure that the President cannot act as a "lone wolf" in foreign policy or fill the government with cronies and extremists.

Under Article II, the President has the power to negotiate treaties, but they do not become law until the Senate concurs by a **two-thirds vote**. This requirement forces the President to consult with Senate leaders during the negotiation process. If a treaty is unpopular or perceived as a threat to national sovereignty, the Senate can reject it entirely, as it famously did with the Treaty of Versailles after World War I. This high threshold makes the United States a stable and predictable partner in international affairs, as any treaty that passes has broad domestic support.

Confirmations cover a vast array of positions, from Supreme Court justices and cabinet secretaries to ambassadors and lower-level federal judges. The Senate Judiciary Committee handles judicial picks, while other committees vet the leaders of the departments they oversee. This process allows the Senate to examine a nominee's qualifications, temperament, and judicial or political philosophy.

The confirmation process has become increasingly contentious in recent decades. The Senate can use a "filibuster" to block a nominee, though both parties have recently utilized the "nuclear option" to change the rules so that most nominees now only require a simple majority vote.

Despite this, the power to confirm remains a massive check. A President whose party does not control the Senate often finds it impossible to fill key vacancies, leaving agencies without permanent leadership.

Senatorial courtesy is an informal custom that further expands this power. If a President is appointing a federal official to serve in a specific state (like a district court judge or a U.S. Attorney), he will usually consult with the senators from that state if they belong to his party. If a senator from the home state objects to the nominee, the rest of the Senate will often refuse to confirm them as a courtesy to their colleague. This gives individual senators a virtual veto over federal appointments in their own backyard.

War Powers

The division of war powers is the most contested territory in the Constitution. Article I grants Congress the power to "declare War," "raise and support Armies," and "provide and maintain a Navy." Meanwhile, Article II names the President as the "Commander in Chief." This creates a deliberate tension: the President directs the troops, but Congress decides if the troops should be fighting and provides the money to sustain them.

For the first 150 years of the republic, this system was relatively clear. Congress issued formal declarations of war for major conflicts. However, since World War II, the United States has fought several major conflicts (including Korea and Vietnam) without a formal declaration. Instead, Congress has often used an **Authorization for Use of Military Force (AUMF)** or simply provided funding for the conflict through appropriations.

In 1973, over President Nixon's veto, Congress passed the **War Powers Resolution** to reassert its authority. This law requires the President to notify Congress within 48 hours of committing armed forces to hostilities. It also mandates that the President withdraw those forces within 60 to 90 days unless Congress explicitly authorizes the action or declares war.

The effectiveness of the War Powers Resolution is a matter of intense debate. Every President since Nixon has argued that the law is an unconstitutional infringement on executive authority. Presidents frequently argue that they have the inherent power to protect national security without prior congressional approval. Congress, for its part, often hesitates to use the law's enforcement mechanisms, fearing the political fallout of "cutting off the troops" while they are in harm's way.

The true power of Congress in wartime remains the power of the purse. Even if a President ignores the War Powers Resolution, he cannot continue a war indefinitely if Congress refuses to pay for it. The legislature can also use "resolutions of inquiry" to force the administration to reveal the goals and costs of a military intervention. While the "commander in chief" role gives the President the first move, the "purse strings" give Congress the final word on the duration and scope of American military engagement.

The Breadth of Authority

These non-legislative powers transform Congress from a mere debating society into a co-equal branch of government. They provide the tools necessary to ensure that the "checks and balances" written on parchment are a reality in practice. Whether it's through the meticulous auditing of a federal budget, the public cross-examination of a cabinet secretary, or the solemn trial of an impeached official, the legislature remains the primary guardian of the constitutional order.

The use of these powers often reflects the political climate. In times of **divided government**, when different parties control the White House and Congress, oversight and investigations tend to be more aggressive. In times of national crisis, the war powers and fiscal authorities come to the forefront. Yet, regardless of the political winds, the existence of these powers ensures that the executive branch remains accountable to the representatives of the people.

The complexity of these authorities also highlights the need for institutional expertise. For Congress to effectively check the President, it must have its own sources of information and a deep understanding of the law. This is why the committee system and the support agencies like the GAO and CBO are so vital. Without them, the non-legislative powers of Congress would be hollow, and the balance of power would shift decisively toward an "imperial presidency."

Congressional authority is a dynamic and evolving force. As the federal government has grown in size and complexity, the ways in which the legislature exercises its oversight and fiscal powers have changed, but the fundamental mission remains the same. The Founders designed a system where no single branch could act alone, and the non-legislative powers of Congress are the glue that holds that system together. They ensure that the government's actions are transparent, its officials are honest, and its spending is authorized by the people's representatives.

Do you believe the increasing use of the "Authorization for Use of Military Force" (AUMF) as a substitute for a formal declaration of war has permanently shifted the balance of power toward the executive branch?

Chapter 12: The Executive Branch and Its Relationship to Congress

The President of the United States holds a position that the Framers intended to be energetic but strictly bounded. Unlike a monarch, the President doesn't possess inherent authority to create law or spend public funds. Instead, the executive branch functions primarily to carry out the will of the legislature. This relationship creates a permanent tension. The President often tries to expand executive reach to address national crises, while Congress guards its constitutional prerogatives with jealousy. This dynamic defines the daily operations of the federal government.

Presidential Election and the Electoral College

The method of choosing the President was one of the most difficult problems the delegates in Philadelphia faced. They didn't trust a direct popular vote, fearing that a "demagogue" might manipulate an uninformed public. They also rejected letting Congress choose the President, as that would make the executive a mere puppet of the legislature.

The solution was the **Electoral College**, a unique and often misunderstood compromise. It creates a buffer between the people and the presidency while balancing the interests of large and small states.

Under this system, each state receives a number of electors equal to its total number of Senators and Representatives. This math guarantees every state at least three electoral votes. There are 538 total electors today: 435 based on House seats, 100 based on Senate seats, and 3 for the District of Columbia. To win the presidency, a candidate must secure a majority of 270 votes.

Most states utilize a "winner-take-all" system. If a candidate wins the popular vote in a state by even a single ballot, they receive all of that state's electoral votes. Maine and Nebraska are the exceptions, using a "district system" that can split their votes. Critics argue this system allows a candidate to win the White House while losing the national popular vote, which has happened five times in American history. Supporters contend it forces candidates to appeal to a broad geographic coalition rather than just focusing on high-population urban centers.

The **12th Amendment** refined this process after the election of 1800 resulted in a tie between Thomas Jefferson and Aaron Burr. Originally, electors cast two votes for President; the runner-up became Vice President. This led to a situation where political rivals were forced to serve together. The amendment changed this, requiring electors to cast separate ballots for President and Vice President. This effectively codified the role of political parties in the executive branch.

If no candidate reaches 270 votes, the election goes to the House of Representatives in what's known as a **contingency election**. In this scenario, each state delegation gets exactly one vote. The House chooses from the top three candidates. This procedure reinforces the federal character of the system, giving equal weight to every state regardless of its population size. It has happened only twice, most notably in 1824 when John Quincy Adams won despite Andrew Jackson having more popular and electoral votes.

Executive Orders and Directives

The President's most visible tool for independent action is the **executive order**. These are formal directives issued by the President to managed the operations of the federal government. While the Constitution doesn't explicitly mention "executive orders," the authority stems from Article II. Specifically, the "executive Power" and the duty to "take Care that the Laws be faithfully executed" provide the legal foundation.

An executive order carries the full force of law, but it isn't a statute. It cannot create new crimes or levy new taxes. Instead, it directs how existing laws are implemented by executive agencies.

For example, if Congress passes a law requiring the military to be integrated, the President issues an executive order to the Department of Defense to carry out that mandate. Over time, Presidents have used these orders for massive policy shifts, such as Harry Truman's desegregation of the armed forces or Franklin Roosevelt's internment of Japanese Americans.

The relationship with Congress here is one of constant checking. Congress can effectively "overrule" an executive order by passing a law that contradicts it or by withholding the funding necessary to carry it out. However, if the President vetoes that law, Congress needs a two-thirds majority to prevail. The Supreme Court also monitors this power. In *Youngstown Sheet & Tube Co. v. Sawyer* (1952), the Court ruled that President Truman couldn't seize private steel mills during a strike, even during the Korean War, because Congress hadn't authorized such an action.

Executive agreements are the foreign policy equivalent of executive orders. These are pacts made between the President and the head of a foreign government. Unlike formal treaties, they don't require a two-thirds vote in the Senate. This allows the President to move quickly on international matters like trade or military cooperation. However, these agreements aren't as legally durable as treaties. A future President can rescind an executive agreement with a stroke of a pen, whereas a treaty remains part of the "supreme Law of the Land" until formally repealed.

Presidential proclamations and **memoranda** serve similar purposes but usually carry less weight. Proclamations are often ceremonial, like declaring a national day of remembrance. Memoranda are informal instructions to agency heads. While they lack the formal numbering of executive orders, they are often just as effective at changing how the government operates on a daily basis.

The Federal Bureaucracy

While the President is the head of the executive branch, they don't work alone. The **federal bureaucracy** consists of roughly 2.1 million civilian employees who perform the actual work of governing. This "fourth branch" is organized into departments, agencies, and commissions. Its primary purpose is implementation: taking the broad goals of Congress and turning them into specific actions.

At the top of the hierarchy are the **15 Cabinet Departments**, such as State, Treasury, and Defense. Each is led by a Secretary appointed by the President and confirmed by the Senate. These departments handle the most significant and traditional functions of government. Below them are **independent executive agencies** like NASA or the EPA. These aren't part of a cabinet department and often have a narrower focus.

Independent regulatory commissions, such as the Federal Communications Commission (FCC) or the Securities and Exchange Commission (SEC), are different. They are designed to be insulated from political pressure. Their leaders serve fixed terms and can't be fired by the President without just cause. This independence ensures that experts, not politicians, make technical decisions about things like radio frequencies or stock market rules.

The civil service has evolved significantly. In the 1800s, the "spoils system" reigned; presidents gave government jobs to their political supporters regardless of ability. This led to massive corruption and inefficiency. The **Pendleton Act of 1883** replaced this with the **merit system**.

Today, most federal employees are hired based on their qualifications and performance on competitive exams. This creates a stable, professional workforce that continues to function even when the presidency changes parties.

The bureaucracy possesses two types of power that often irritate Congress: **administrative discretion** and **rule-making**. Administrative discretion is the authority of bureaucrats to choose the best way to implement a law. Since Congress often writes vague laws, the bureaucracy must fill in the blanks. This leads to the "administrative state," where unelected officials make decisions that affect millions of people every day.

Agency Rulemaking and Congressional Review

When an agency like the Occupational Safety and Health Administration (OSHA) wants to create a new safety standard, it doesn't just write a memo. It follows a formal process called **rulemaking**, governed by the **Administrative Procedure Act (APA)** of 1946. This law ensures that the public and Congress have a say in how agencies exercise their delegated power.

The most common method is "notice-and-comment" rulemaking.

1. The agency publishes a "Notice of Proposed Rulemaking" in the **Federal Register**.

2. Interested parties, lobbyists, and citizens have a specific period (usually 30 to 90 days) to submit written comments.
3. The agency must read and respond to these comments in the final rule.
4. The final rule is published and has the force of law.

This process is where the executive branch acts most like a legislature. These rules are often thousands of pages long and carry significant economic consequences. Because the bureaucrats making these rules aren't elected, Congress keeps them on a short leash through **congressional oversight**. Committees hold hearings to grill agency heads about proposed rules, and the Government Accountability Office (GAO) audits their effectiveness.

The **Congressional Review Act (CRA)** of 1996 provides a more direct check. It requires agencies to submit all new "major" rules to Congress before they take effect. If both the House and the Senate pass a "joint resolution of disapproval" and the President signs it (or Congress overrides a veto), the rule is nullified. Furthermore, if a rule is struck down under the CRA, the agency is prohibited from ever issuing a "substantially similar" rule in the future.

The "insider" relationship between a congressional committee, an executive agency, and an interest group is known as an **Iron Triangle**. These three groups often work together to protect a specific policy or program, sometimes at the expense of the general public. For example, a committee that oversees agriculture, the Department of Agriculture, and the dairy lobby might work in unison to keep milk subsidies high. Breaking these triangles is difficult because each member of the group benefits from the status quo.

Checks on Executive Authority

The President's relationship with Congress isn't just about rulemaking; it's about the fundamental balance of power. The Constitution gives Congress the "power of the purse," meaning the President can't spend money that hasn't been appropriated. If the President wants to build a border wall or launch a new healthcare initiative, they must convince Congress to pay for it. This financial dependence is the most effective check on executive ambition.

Impeachment, covered earlier, remains the ultimate deterrent. The House can impeach a President for "Treason, Bribery, or other high Crimes and Misdemeanors," and the Senate can remove them with a two-thirds vote. While rare, the mere threat of impeachment can force a President to change course or resign, as seen with Richard Nixon. It reminds the President that they are a citizen-executive, not a king.

The judicial branch also plays a role through **judicial review**. Federal courts can strike down executive orders or agency rules that violate the Constitution or exceed the authority granted by Congress. In recent years, the Supreme Court has invoked the "major questions doctrine" to limit agency power. This principle states that if an agency wants to decide an issue of "vast economic and political significance," it must have clear and specific authorization from Congress. It cannot rely on vague, old laws to claim new and sweeping powers.

Action	Executive Authority	Congressional Check
Appointing a Cabinet Secretary	President chooses nominee	Senate must confirm (Advice and Consent)
Spending on a New Program	President proposes budget	Congress must pass appropriations bill
Making a Trade Deal	President signs Executive Agreement	Congress can pass law to override or defund
Issuing a National Regulation	Agency conducts rulemaking	Congress can use CRA to nullify

The executive branch is significantly more powerful today than it was in 1789. The growth of the national economy and the emergence of the United States as a global superpower have necessitated a more active presidency.

However, the structural limits remain. The President is a coordinator and a manager, bound by the statutes passed by Congress and the interpretations handed down by the courts. This interdependence means that the government can't move too quickly in any one direction without broad consensus. The President might have the "bully pulpit" to speak to the nation, but they need the "legislative engine" of Congress to turn those words into permanent policy. This friction was the primary goal of the Founders. They wanted a government that required cooperation between the branches to achieve any significant goal.

The bureaucracy serves as the connective tissue of this system. It provides the expertise that Congress lacks and the manpower that the President needs. While it is often criticized for being slow and "faceless," it ensures that the laws are applied consistently across the entire nation. The merit-based civil service prevents the federal government from becoming a tool for political vengeance, maintaining a level of professionalism that is vital for a functioning republic.

Ultimately, the executive branch is defined by its relationship to the other two branches. It cannot exist in a vacuum. Every presidential action, from an offhand tweet to a formal executive order, is weighed against the constitutional powers of Congress and the legal standards of the judiciary. This constant oversight prevents the "energetic executive" from becoming a "tyrannical executive." The balance is delicate, but it has survived for over two centuries.

Do you think the "major questions doctrine" is an essential tool for reasserting congressional authority, or does it prevent the executive branch from effectively responding to modern crises that the Founders couldn't have envisioned?

Chapter 13: The Judicial Branch and Constitutional Interpretation

Alexander Hamilton famously described the judiciary as the "least dangerous branch" because it possesses neither the "sword" of the executive nor the "purse" of the legislature. It cannot command armies or levy taxes. It relies entirely on the other branches to enforce its rulings and on the public's perception of its legitimacy. Yet, in modern American life, the judicial branch often serves as the final arbiter of our most profound social, political, and economic disputes. From the legality of healthcare mandates to the definition of marriage and the limits of presidential immunity, the courts hold a power that is both immense and fragile.

Structure of the Federal Courts

The federal judiciary operates as a three-tiered pyramid. Article III of the Constitution establishes the Supreme Court but leaves the creation of "inferior" courts to Congress. This flexibility allowed the system to grow from a handful of judges in 1789 to the expansive network that exists today.

At the base of the pyramid are the **U.S. District Courts**. These are the trial courts of the federal system. There are currently 94 district courts spread across the fifty states, the District of Columbia, and U.S. territories. This is where federal cases begin. When the government prosecutes a federal crime or a citizen sues for a violation of civil rights, the proceedings happen here. District courts utilize juries to determine the facts of a case, and a single judge presides over the application of the law.

The middle tier consists of the **U.S. Courts of Appeals**, often called circuit courts. The nation is divided into 12 regional circuits, with a 13th "Federal Circuit" that handles specialized cases like patents and international trade. These are strictly appellate courts. They do not hold trials, hear new evidence, or use juries. Instead, a panel of three judges reviews the record from the district court to determine if the legal procedures were followed correctly. If you lose at the district level, you have an automatic right to appeal to the circuit court.

At the apex stands the **Supreme Court of the United States** (SCOTUS). It is primarily an appellate court, meaning it hears cases that have already worked their way through the lower tiers or through the state court systems. Unlike the circuit courts, the Supreme Court is not required to hear every case. It exercises "discretionary jurisdiction," choosing which disputes are significant enough to warrant its attention. The decisions made here are final and binding on every other court in the country.

(The Supreme Court shapes national policy through constitutional interpretation, often resolving conflicts between federal authority and individual rights. Its influence extends beyond individual cases, as rulings set binding precedent that guides future decisions. Through concepts like the writ of certiorari and majority opinions, it controls its docket and frames legal doctrine. Concurring and dissenting opinions signal future legal shifts.)

Federal courts are courts of "limited jurisdiction." They cannot hear every dispute. To get into federal court, a case must usually involve a "federal question" (matters involving the Constitution, federal laws, or treaties) or "diversity of citizenship" (disputes between citizens of different states involving more than 75,000 dollars). This is so that federal judges don't overwhelm state courts, which handle the vast majority of day-to-day legal business like contracts, torts, and family law.

Supreme Court Jurisdiction

The Supreme Court's authority is divided into two categories: **original jurisdiction** and **appellate jurisdiction**. Original jurisdiction refers to cases that start at the Supreme Court. According to Article III, these involve "Ambassadors, other public Ministers and Consuls, and those in which a State shall be Party." Most commonly today, this involves lawsuits between two states over water rights or boundary lines. These cases are rare; the Court often appoints a "Special Master" to gather evidence and make recommendations before the justices vote.

The vast majority of the Court's workload falls under appellate jurisdiction. Each year, thousands of litigants file a **petition for a writ of certiorari**, asking the Court to review their case. The justices and their clerks review these petitions to identify "cert-worthy" cases. These usually involve a "circuit split," where different federal appeals courts have interpreted the same law in different ways, or cases that present a "substantial federal question" of national importance.

The Court operates under the **Rule of Four**. If four of the nine justices agree that a case warrants review, the Court grants "cert" and schedules the case for oral argument. This rule protects the minority of the Court, allowing them to bring issues to the floor even if the majority might eventually rule against them.

Legal Term	Definition
Writ of Certiorari	A formal order by the Supreme Court to a lower court to send up the record of a case for review.
Amicus Curiae	"Friend of the court" briefs filed by outside groups to provide information or arguments on a case.
Stare Decisis	The principle of following precedent; letting the previous decision stand.
Remand	When a higher court sends a case back to a lower court for further action.

Oral arguments are a unique spectacle. Each side usually receives only thirty minutes to present its case. The justices frequently interrupt with questions, testing the logic of the attorneys' positions. Following arguments, the justices meet in a private "conference" to discuss and vote. The Chief Justice, if in the majority, assigns the writing of the **majority opinion**. If the Chief is in the minority, the most senior justice in the majority makes the assignment. This opinion is the most important output of the Court, as it sets the legal precedent that all lower courts must follow.

Justices who disagree with the majority may write a **dissenting opinion**. While dissents have no legal force, they serve as a roadmap for future challenges and can eventually influence the Court to overturn its own precedent.

A **concurring opinion** is written by a justice who agrees with the outcome of the case but for different legal reasons. These multiple opinions often reveal the deep philosophical divisions within the Court.

Judicial Appointments and Confirmation

Federal judges hold their offices "during good Behavior," which effectively means life tenure. The only way to remove a federal judge is through impeachment by the House and conviction by the Senate. This was a deliberate choice by the Framers to ensure **judicial independence**. If a judge doesn't have to worry about being fired or losing an election, they can make unpopular decisions that are legally correct without fearing political retribution.

The appointment process is a two-step dance between the President and the Senate. The President nominates a candidate, and the Senate provides "Advice and Consent." For district court positions, the President often follows the tradition of **senatorial courtesy**, consulting with the senators from the state where the judge will serve. For the Supreme Court, the process is intensely national and highly partisan.

The Senate Judiciary Committee conducts hearings where the nominee is questioned about their legal career, judicial philosophy, and past rulings. These hearings have become increasingly contentious.

The failed 1987 nomination of Robert Bork changed the landscape, as interest groups began spending millions of dollars to support or oppose nominees based on their perceived ideological leanings. "Borking" became a verb meaning to systematically attack a candidate's character or philosophy to block their confirmation.

Once the committee approves a nominee, the full Senate votes. For most of American history, a "filibuster" could block a nominee, requiring sixty votes to move to a final vote. However, in 2013, the Democrats eliminated the filibuster for lower-court nominees. In 2017, Republicans did the same for Supreme Court nominees. Today, a simple majority of 51 votes is all that's required to seat a justice. This has made the process more streamlined but also more partisan, as the majority party no longer needs to find a candidate who can appeal to the opposition.

Life tenure combined with the power of judicial review makes these appointments the longest-lasting legacy of any president. A president might serve four or eight years, but their judicial picks can influence American law for thirty or forty years. This reality has turned the Supreme Court into a central issue in presidential campaigns, with voters often casting ballots based on which candidate will appoint justices who align with their views on abortion, gun rights, or executive power.

Marbury v. Madison and Judicial Review

The Constitution does not explicitly grant the Supreme Court the power to strike down laws. That authority, known as **judicial review**, was established by the Court itself in the 1803 case ***Marbury v. Madison***. This case is the most significant in American history because it defined the judiciary as a co-equal branch of government capable of checking the actions of both Congress and the President.

The dispute arose from the "midnight appointments" of outgoing President John Adams. In his final days in office, Adams appointed several new judges, including William Marbury. However, the formal commissions were not delivered before Thomas Jefferson took office. Jefferson ordered his Secretary of State, James Madison, to withhold the commissions. Marbury sued, asking the Supreme Court to issue a "writ of mandamus" to force Madison to deliver his job.

Chief Justice **John Marshall** faced a political dilemma. If he ordered the commission delivered, Jefferson would likely ignore the Court, making the judiciary look weak. If he refused, it would look like he was caving to the executive branch.

Marshall's solution was a stroke of legal genius. He ruled that while Marbury was entitled to his commission, the law that gave the Supreme Court the power to hear the case (the Judiciary Act of 1789) was unconstitutional because it expanded the Court's original jurisdiction beyond what Article III allowed.

By striking down a federal law for the first time, Marshall established that "It is emphatically the province and duty of the judicial department to say what the law is." He argued that the Constitution is a superior law that limits the power of the government. If a law passed by Congress conflicts with the Constitution, the law must be void. Marbury lost his job, but the Supreme Court won the power to be the final guardian of the constitutional order.

Judicial review isn't just about federal laws. In *Martin v. Hunter's Lessee* (1816) and *Cohens v. Virginia* (1821), the Marshall Court established that it also has the power to review state court decisions and state laws so that they comply with the Constitution. This established the Supreme Court as the unifying force in the American legal system, preventing thirteen (and later fifty) different interpretations of federal law.

Originalism versus Living Constitutionalism

How should a judge interpret a document written in 1787 and amended only a handful of times?

This question divides the legal community into two primary camps: **Originalism** and **Living Constitutionalism**. These aren't just academic theories; they determine how rights are defined in the modern era.

Originalism argues that the Constitution should be interpreted according to its original public meaning at the time it was adopted. Originalists, like the late Justice Antonin Scalia or Justice Clarence Thomas, believe that the text is a fixed anchor. They argue that if the meaning of the Constitution can change with the whims of judges, the document is no longer a "law" but a political tool. If the people want the Constitution to mean something different, the originalist argument goes, they should amend it through the process in Article V.

Within originalism, there is a distinction between **Original Intent** (what the Framers specifically wanted) and **Original Public Meaning** (how a reasonable person at the time would have understood the words). Most modern originalists focus on public meaning. For example, when interpreting the Second Amendment, an originalist looks at 18th-century dictionaries and legal treatises to understand what "keep and bear arms" meant to the generation that ratified the Bill of Rights.

Living Constitutionalism, or the "Living Constitution" theory, argues that the document must be interpreted in light of evolving social values and circumstances. Proponents, like the late Justice Ruth Bader Ginsburg or Justice Stephen Breyer, argue that the Framers used broad, majestic language like "due process" and "equal protection" precisely because they wanted the document to endure and adapt. They contend that an 18th-century understanding of "cruel and unusual punishment" shouldn't limit our ability to regulate modern prisons or the death penalty.

Living constitutionalists often prioritize the "spirit" or "purpose" of a provision over its literal 1787 meaning. They argue that originalism is often used as a cloak for conservative politics and that it is impossible to truly know the minds of people who lived 250 years ago. Originalists counter that living constitutionalism allows unelected judges to act as a "super-legislature," creating new rights (like the right to privacy) that aren't mentioned in the text.

Landmark Constitutional Cases

The history of the Supreme Court is a history of the nation's most difficult choices. A "landmark" case is one that fundamentally changes our understanding of the law or the relationship between the citizen and the state. These cases often reflect the era in which they were decided, showing how the Court's philosophy has shifted over time.

***McCulloch v. Maryland* (1819):** This case established the doctrine of **implied powers**. The Court ruled that Congress had the authority to create a national bank even though "bank" isn't in the Constitution. Marshall used the "Necessary and Proper Clause" to argue that the federal government has the power to use any appropriate means to carry out its enumerated ends. It also reinforced federal supremacy by ruling that Maryland could not tax a federal institution.

***Dred Scott v. Sandford* (1857):** Widely considered the Court's greatest failure. Chief Justice Roger Taney ruled that Black people, whether enslaved or free, could never be citizens of the United States and had "no rights which the white man was bound to respect." The Court also struck down the Missouri Compromise, ruling that Congress had no power to prohibit slavery in the territories. This decision accelerated the move toward the Civil War and was eventually overturned by the 14th Amendment.

***Plessy v. Ferguson* (1896) and *Brown v. Board of Education* (1954):** These cases represent the Court's pivot on racial equality. *Plessy* established the "separate but equal" doctrine, allowing states to maintain racially segregated facilities. Decades later, the Court unanimously overturned *Plessy* in *Brown*, ruling that "separate educational facilities are inherently unequal." *Brown* was a turning point for the Civil Rights Movement and demonstrated the Court's power to correct its own past errors.

***Gideon v. Wainwright* (1963) and *Miranda v. Arizona* (1966):** These cases expanded the rights of the accused. *Gideon* established that the 6th Amendment requires states to provide an attorney to any defendant who cannot afford one. *Miranda* required police to inform suspects of their rights before interrogation. These rulings ensured that the protections of the Bill of Rights are a reality for everyone, not just those who know the law or can afford a lawyer. They also accelerated the incorporation of constitutional protections against the states through the 14th Amendment, standardizing criminal procedure nationwide. In practice, they shifted power at the point of arrest and trial, forcing law enforcement and courts to operate within clearer constitutional boundaries.

***Roe v. Wade* (1973) and *Dobbs v. Jackson Women's Health Organization* (2022):** These cases highlight the ongoing battle over "substantive due process" and unwritten rights. *Roe* established a constitutional right to abortion based on a right to privacy found in the "penumbras" of the Bill of Rights. Nearly fifty years later, the Court in *Dobbs* took the extraordinary step of overhauling that precedent. The majority argued that because the Constitution doesn't mention abortion and the right isn't "deeply rooted in the nation's history," it isn't a constitutional right. This returned the issue to the states and sparked a massive debate over the stability of precedent (*stare decisis*).

***Obergefell v. Hodges* (2015):** The Court ruled that the 14th Amendment requires states to license and recognize same-sex marriages. This decision was a triumph for living constitutionalism, with the majority arguing that the meaning of "liberty" and "equal protection" must grow to include groups previously excluded from fundamental rights. The dissenters, sticking to an originalist or traditionalist view, argued that the Court was usurping the role of the democratic process.

The Role of Precedent and Change

The Supreme Court is a conservative institution by nature, meaning it is slow to change. The principle of **stare decisis** ("to stand by things decided") is the default position. Judges generally follow past rulings to ensure the law remains predictable and stable. If the law changed every time a new justice was appointed, no one would know what their rights were from one year to the next.

However, precedent is not an "inexorable command." The Court can and does overturn itself when it believes a past decision was "egregiously wrong." The shift from *Plessy* to *Brown* or from *Roe* to *Dobbs* shows that the Court is a human institution, influenced by the shifting legal arguments and philosophies of the people who sit on the bench.

The tension between stability and change is the core of the judicial branch's work. The justices must balance the need for a consistent legal framework with the need to ensure the Constitution remains relevant to a modern, diverse society.

This balance is maintained through the rigorous process of written opinions, where every justice must justify their reasoning to the public, the legal community, and future generations.

The "Least Dangerous" Branch?

Is the judiciary still the least dangerous branch? In many ways, its power has surpassed what the Founders imagined. The ability to strike down an act of Congress or a presidential order with a five-to-four vote gives the Court a massive influence over national policy. Because the justices serve for life, they are the only part of the government that doesn't have to answer to the voters.

Yet, Hamilton's assessment remains true in one fundamental way: the Court has no power to enforce its own rulings. When the Court ordered the desegregation of schools in *Brown*, it took over a decade and the intervention of the President and Congress to make that order a reality in many parts of the country. If the public loses faith in the Court's impartiality, or if the other branches decide to ignore its rulings, the Court's authority disappears.

The legitimacy of the Supreme Court depends on the perception that it is a court of law, not a court of politics. When the confirmation process becomes a partisan circus, or when the Court overturns long-standing precedents on ideological lines, that legitimacy is threatened. The ongoing debate over "court-packing" (increasing the number of justices to change the ideological balance) or term limits for justices reflects a growing concern that the "least dangerous branch" has become too central to our political combat.

The judicial branch is the anchor of the American system. It provides the final word on what the rules are and ensures that those rules apply to everyone, including the government itself.

As the nation continues to debate the meaning of its founding document, the courts will remain the arena where our most fundamental values are tested and refined. The "greatest experiment" in self-government depends on a judiciary that can remain independent, principled, and respected.

Do you believe that life tenure for federal judges is still the best way to ensure judicial independence, or has it led to a system where the stakes of every appointment are too high for a healthy democracy?

Chapter 14: Civil Liberties and Civil Rights

The distinction between civil liberties and civil rights is a fundamental requirement for understanding American governance. While the terms often appear together in political discourse, they represent two different types of constitutional protections. Civil liberties are the individual freedoms that the government cannot legally take away, largely found in the Bill of Rights. They are the "thou shalt nots" that limit the reach of federal and state authority. Civil rights, conversely, involve the government's obligation to ensure that people are treated equally and protected from discrimination. If liberties are about freedom, rights are about equality.

The American experiment relies on the constant negotiation between these two pillars. The Constitution provides a framework where the majority cannot simply vote away the fundamental freedoms of the minority. Over two centuries, the definition of who "the people" are has expanded, and the scope of what the government must protect has deepened.

This evolution hasn't been a smooth, linear progression; it has been a series of hard-fought legal and political battles that continue to shape the daily lives of every citizen.

Free Speech and Press Protections

The First Amendment begins with a clear prohibition: "Congress shall make no law... abridging the freedom of speech, or of the press." This command serves as the bedrock of a self-governing society. If citizens cannot criticize their leaders, share information, or debate ideas without fear of imprisonment, democracy cannot function. The Founders viewed a free press as a "watchdog" that exposes corruption and keeps the public informed.

However, the right to free speech has never been absolute. The government can limit speech that poses a direct threat to national security or public safety, though the bar for doing so is incredibly high. In the early twentieth century, the Supreme Court used the "clear and present danger" test to determine when the government could interfere. Today, the standard is much stricter. In ***Brandenburg v. Ohio*** (1969), the Court ruled that the government cannot punish inflammatory speech unless it is directed to inciting or producing "imminent lawless action" and is likely to produce such action. This protection extends even to hateful or deeply offensive speech, based on the theory that the best remedy for bad speech is "more speech," not censorship.

The press enjoys a specific protection against **prior restraint**, which is government action that prohibits speech or other expression before it can take place. In the landmark "Pentagon Papers" case (***New York Times Co. v. United States***, 1971), the Nixon administration attempted to stop the publication of classified documents about the Vietnam War. The Supreme Court ruled against the government, asserting that any attempt at prior restraint carries a heavy presumption of unconstitutionality. Unless the government can prove that publication will cause immediate, irreparable harm to the nation, the press has the right to publish.

Symbolic speech is also protected. This includes non-verbal actions that convey a political message, such as wearing an armband or burning a flag. In ***Tinker v. Des Moines*** (1969), the Court famously declared that students do not "shed their constitutional rights to freedom of speech or expression at the schoolhouse gate." While schools can limit speech that causes a substantial disruption to the educational environment, they can't suppress student expression simply because the message is unpopular or controversial.

Another major dimension of First Amendment doctrine is the distinction between content-based and content-neutral regulations. When the government targets speech because of its message, viewpoint, or subject matter, courts apply strict scrutiny, the highest level of judicial review. This means the government must prove the law serves a compelling interest and is narrowly tailored to achieve that goal.

By contrast, content-neutral regulations, such as limits on the time, place, and manner of expression, are more easily upheld so long as they are reasonable and leave open alternative channels for communication.

The Court has also identified specific categories of speech that receive little or no constitutional protection. These include true threats, obscenity, defamation, and fighting words. Even here, the definitions are tightly constrained. For example, defamation requires false statements of fact that harm a person's reputation, and public figures must meet a higher standard by proving "actual malice," meaning the speaker knew the statement was false or acted with reckless disregard for the truth.

In the modern era, digital platforms have complicated the application of free speech principles. Social media allows individuals to reach massive audiences instantly, blurring the line between private and public forums.

While the First Amendment restricts government action, not private companies, debates continue over how platform moderation affects the practical scope of free expression. These developments show that while the core principles remain stable, their application continues to evolve alongside technology and changing forms of communication.

Religious Freedom and Establishment

The Constitution addresses religion through two distinct clauses in the First Amendment: the **Establishment Clause** and the **Free Exercise Clause**. Together, they create what Thomas Jefferson called a "wall of separation" between church and state. The goal was to prevent the kind of religious conflict that had plagued Europe for centuries, ensuring that the government neither promotes a specific faith nor prohibits the practice of religion.

The Establishment Clause prohibits the government from creating a national religion or favoring one religion over another. For decades, the Supreme Court used the "Lemon Test" (from ***Lemon v. Kurtzman***, 1971) to determine if a government action violated this clause. To be constitutional, a law had to have a secular purpose, neither advance nor inhibit religion, and avoid "excessive government entanglement" with religion. In recent years, the Court has shifted toward a more "accommodationist" approach, allowing more room for religious expression in the public square as long as it isn't coercive.

The Free Exercise Clause protects a citizen's right to practice their religion as they see fit. This includes the right to believe whatever one chooses and, to a large extent, the right to act on those beliefs. Conflict arises when a religious practice clashes with a general law. In ***Wisconsin v. Yoder*** (1972), the Court ruled that Amish families could not be forced to send their children to public school past the eighth grade, as it would violate their fundamental religious tenets.

However, religious belief does not provide a blank check to ignore the law. The government can limit religious practices if it has a "compelling interest" and uses the "least restrictive means" to achieve it. For example, the government can prohibit polygamy or the use of illegal drugs in religious ceremonies, even if those practices are central to a person's faith. The challenge for the courts is constantly determining where an individual's right to practice their faith ends and the government's duty to maintain a neutral, orderly society begins.

Due Process and Equal Protection

The Fourteenth Amendment is arguably the most important addition to the Constitution since the Bill of Rights. It contains two clauses that have fundamentally transformed the American legal landscape: the **Due Process Clause** and the **Equal Protection Clause**. These provisions bridged the gap between the idealistic promises of the Declaration of Independence and the practical reality of American law.

Due process comes in two forms: procedural and substantive. Procedural due process is the requirement that the government follow fair methods before depriving a person of life, liberty, or property. This includes the right to a notice, a hearing, and an impartial judge. It means that the "machinery" of the law isn't used arbitrarily.

Substantive due process is more complex; it suggests that there are certain fundamental rights that the government cannot infringe upon at all, regardless of the procedures it follows. This has been the basis for rights not explicitly listed in the Constitution, such as the right to privacy and the right to marry.

The Equal Protection Clause mandates that "no State shall... deny to any person within its jurisdiction the equal protection of the laws." This is the primary tool for fighting discrimination. When the government treats one group of people differently than another, the courts apply different levels of "scrutiny" to determine if the law is constitutional.

Level of Scrutiny	Application	Government Requirement
Strict Scrutiny	Race, national origin, religion	Must prove a "compelling interest" and "narrow tailoring"
Intermediate Scrutiny	Gender	Must prove an "important objective"
Rational Basis	Age, wealth, sexual orientation (historically)	Must prove the law is "rationally related" to a legitimate goal

Strict scrutiny is the highest hurdle. If a law discriminates based on race, it is almost always found unconstitutional. This was the logic behind ***Brown v. Board of Education*** (1954), which struck down the "separate but equal" doctrine in public schools. The Court ruled that state-sanctioned segregation created an inherent sense of inferiority that violated the Equal Protection Clause. This decision didn't just end school segregation; it provided the legal foundation for the entire Civil Rights Movement, leading to the dismantling of Jim Crow laws across the country.

Equal protection also applies to the legislative process itself. The government cannot pass laws that are intentionally designed to harm a specific group of people without a valid, non-discriminatory reason.

While the Fourteenth Amendment originally focused on protecting the rights of formerly enslaved people, it has been expanded to protect women, the disabled, and the LGBTQ+ community. Each expansion reflects a growing national consensus that the law must treat every citizen with equal dignity.

Voting Rights Expansion

The original Constitution said remarkably little about who had the right to vote. It left the determination of voter qualifications entirely to the states. In the early 1800s, this meant that in most places, only white, male, property-owning citizens could cast a ballot. The history of American democracy is characterized by a steady, often violent, expansion of the **franchise** to include those previously excluded.

This expansion occurred through both constitutional amendments and federal legislation. The **15th Amendment** (1870) prohibited denying the right to vote based on race, color, or previous condition of servitude. However, for nearly a century, Southern states used literacy tests, poll taxes, and intimidation to effectively disenfranchise Black voters. It wasn't until the **Voting Rights Act of 1965** that the federal government took an active role in overseeing elections to ensure these discriminatory practices were abolished.

Other amendments continued the trend. The **19th Amendment** (1920) guaranteed women the right to vote after decades of tireless advocacy by the suffrage movement.

The **24th Amendment** (1964) outlawed poll taxes in federal elections, removing a significant economic barrier for poor citizens. Finally, the **26th Amendment** (1971) lowered the voting age from 21 to 18, driven by the argument that if eighteen-year-olds were old enough to be drafted to fight in the Vietnam War, they were old enough to have a say in the government that sent them there.

Today, the battle over voting rights has shifted to issues of election administration and access. Debates over voter ID laws, the location of polling places, and the availability of mail-in ballots are the modern front lines.

Proponents of stricter rules argue they are necessary to preserve "election integrity" and prevent fraud. Opponents argue these rules are modern-day barriers that disproportionately affect minority, elderly, and low-income voters.

Voting is the most fundamental civil right because it is the "right protective of all other rights." Without the ability to choose their representatives, citizens have no way to hold the government accountable for violations of their liberties. The expansion of the electorate has made the American government more representative, but it has also made the political process more complex. Making sure that every eligible citizen can cast a ballot, and that every ballot is counted fairly, remains one of the most persistent challenges in American governance.

The tension between individual liberty and collective rights is never settled. As technology changes and society evolves, new questions arise. Does the Fourth Amendment protect your digital data the same way it protects your physical papers? Does the Equal Protection Clause require "affirmative action" to correct past injustices, or does it mandate a strictly "colorblind" approach? These aren't just legal questions; they are debates about the soul of the nation.

The Bill of Rights and the Fourteenth Amendment provide the tools to address these questions, but they don't provide the final answers. Those answers come from the people, through their representatives, their courts, and their votes. The "blessings of liberty" mentioned in the Preamble are not a static inheritance; they are a project that every generation must renew and protect. The strength of the American system is its ability to adapt its foundational principles to meet the challenges of an ever-changing world.

Does the modern shift toward "originalism" in the Supreme Court threaten to roll back the decades of progress made in expanding civil rights through the "living constitution" interpretation of the Fourteenth Amendment?

Chapter 15: Interest Groups, Parties, and Political Influence

The formal structures of the American government (the Congress, the Presidency, and the Courts) don't operate in a vacuum. They respond to a constant stream of external pressures, demands, and information.

These external forces find their voice through **linkage institutions**, which serve as the connective tissue between the private citizen and the public official. Political parties, interest groups, and the media translate the messy, conflicting desires of 330 million people into a manageable political agenda. Without these organizations, the government would lack the necessary data to make informed policy decisions, and voters would lack the organization to hold their leaders accountable.

Political Party Development

The American Founders viewed political parties with deep suspicion. George Washington's Farewell Address famously warned against the "baneful effects of the spirit of party," which he believed would distract public councils and enfeeble the public administration.

Despite this warning, parties emerged almost immediately because they solved a practical problem: how to organize a diverse group of legislators and voters to achieve a common goal. This development was not a sudden event; it was a gradual evolution from informal factions to the sophisticated, national organizations we see today.

The **First Party System** grew out of the cabinet conflicts between Alexander Hamilton and Thomas Jefferson. The **Federalists**, led by Hamilton, advocated for a strong central government, a national bank, and a commercial economy. The **Democratic-Republicans**, led by Jefferson and James Madison, championed state sovereignty, agrarian interests, and a strict interpretation of the Constitution. This initial divide established the two-party pattern that has dominated American history. Because of the "winner-take-all" nature of the Electoral College and single-member districts, third parties have historically struggled to gain a foothold. This phenomenon, known as **Duverger's Law**, suggests that plurality-rule elections within single-member districts tend to result in a two-party system.

By the 1830s, the **Second Party System** emerged as the Democratic-Republicans split. Andrew Jackson led the newly formed **Democrats**, who focused on expanding the franchise to all white men and dismantling the Second Bank of the United States. His opponents formed the **Whig Party**, which mirrored the earlier Federalist desire for internal improvements and a more active federal role in the economy. This era introduced the "national convention" as a way to nominate candidates, shifting power from a handful of elites in Washington to state-level party leaders.

The issue of slavery eventually destroyed the Whigs and led to the **Third Party System**. The **Republican Party** (GOP) formed in 1854 as a "one-issue" party dedicated to stopping the expansion of slavery into new territories. Following the Civil War, the GOP became the party of the North and the expanding industrial economy, while the Democrats remained the dominant force in the "Solid South."

This era was characterized by **party machines**, urban organizations that provided services to immigrants and the poor in exchange for votes. These machines were often corrupt, but they integrated millions of new citizens into the political process.

Political scientists track the health of parties through **realignments**, rare moments when the core coalitions of the parties shift and the "majority" party changes. The most significant realignment occurred in 1932 during the Great Depression. Franklin D. Roosevelt built the **New Deal Coalition**, bringing together labor unions, Southern whites, Northern Black voters, and urban immigrants under the Democratic banner. This coalition dominated American politics for thirty-six years. A subsequent shift began in 1968, as Southern whites moved toward the GOP in response to the Civil Rights Movement and the "Great Society" programs. This transition led to the modern era of **divided government**, where the presidency and Congress are frequently controlled by different parties.

Today, we are witnessing a period of **dealignment**, where an increasing number of voters identify as "Independent." However, most independents still "lean" toward one party and vote with near-total consistency. While the formal party organizations have weakened because of direct primaries and the rise of candidate-centered campaigns, partisan polarization has reached its highest level in a century.

Voters no longer just disagree with the opposing party; they increasingly view them as a threat to the nation's survival. This "affective polarization" makes compromise in Washington nearly impossible, as any cooperation with the other side is viewed as a betrayal by the party base.

Lobbying and Advocacy

If parties are built to win elections, **interest groups** are built to influence policy. An interest group is any organization of people with shared policy goals who enter the political process to achieve those objectives. Unlike parties, interest groups do not run their own candidates for office; they support candidates who agree with their specific agenda. This distinction is vital. Interest groups are policy specialists, whereas parties are policy generalists. A group like the National Rifle Association (NRA) or the Sierra Club doesn't care about the entire federal budget; they care about how specific sections of that budget affect their core interests.

Lobbying is the primary method interest groups use to influence the government. The term refers to the practice of meeting with officials in the "lobbies" of legislative halls to press a case. Modern lobbying is a multi-billion-dollar industry involving thousands of professional advocates. Most successful lobbyists are experts in their fields, providing legislators with technical data and political intelligence that they cannot easily find elsewhere. A senator voting on a complex telecommunications bill often relies on lobbyists to explain how a specific provision will affect service in their home state.

Lobbyists engage in both "inside" and "outside" strategies. An inside strategy involves direct contact with policymakers, such as testifying at committee hearings, helping to draft legislation, and providing "talking points" for floor debates. An outside strategy (or **grassroots lobbying**) focuses on mobilizing the public to pressure the government. This includes mass email campaigns, social media blitzes, and organized protests. When a thousand constituents call a representative's office on the same day about a specific bill, that representative takes notice.

One of the most controversial aspects of this influence is the **revolving door**. This occurs when former members of Congress or executive branch officials leave the government to become high-priced lobbyists. These individuals sell their "access" and their intimate knowledge of the legislative process to the highest bidder. While there are laws requiring a "cooling-off" period before a former official can lobby their old colleagues, the practice remains a major concern for those worried about the integrity of the government. Critics argue that this creates a system where the government responds to the needs of the wealthy and well-connected rather than the general public.

Interest groups also use the judicial branch through **litigation**. If a group fails to get a law passed in Congress, they may sue in federal court to challenge existing regulations. They often file **amicus curiae** ("friend of the court") briefs to provide the justices with specialized information on a case. Groups like the ACLU or the NAACP have used litigation for decades to achieve policy goals that were politically impossible in the legislature. This "legal advocacy" ensures that even groups without a majority in Congress can still influence the national agenda.

Campaign Finance Regulation

In a democratic republic, the relationship between money and speech is a source of permanent tension. Running a modern political campaign is prohibitively expensive, requiring millions of dollars for television advertising, data analytics, and professional staff.

This creates a dependency: candidates need money to get their message to the voters, and those who provide the money often expect a seat at the table when policy is made. The history of **campaign finance regulation** is a century-long attempt to limit the corrupting influence of large donations without violating the First Amendment right to free expression.

The modern era of regulation began with the **Federal Election Campaign Act (FECA)** of 1971 and its 1974 amendments. This law created the **Federal Election Commission (FEC)** to enforce campaign laws and required candidates to disclose where their money came from and how it was spent. It also established "hard money" limits, which are direct contributions to a candidate's campaign. The Supreme Court reviewed this law in the landmark case ***Buckley v. Valeo*** (1976).

The Court ruled that while the government could limit direct contributions to prevent corruption, it could not limit how much of their own money a candidate spent. The justices famously reasoned that "money is speech" in the context of a political campaign.

This ruling led to the rise of **soft money**, which were unregulated donations to political parties for "party-building activities" like voter registration drives. These funds quickly became a massive loophole, allowing wealthy donors to give millions to parties that were then used to support specific candidates indirectly. To close this loophole,

Congress passed the **Bipartisan Campaign Reform Act (BCRA)** of 2002, also known as the McCain-Feingold Act. This law banned soft money at the national level and prohibited corporations and unions from running "issue ads" (advertisements that mention a candidate by name) in the weeks leading up to an election.

The Supreme Court fundamentally altered this landscape in 2010 with the case ***Citizens United v. FEC***. The Court ruled five-to-four that the government cannot restrict independent expenditures by corporations and unions. The majority argued that these organizations are "associations of people" and therefore possess First Amendment rights. While corporations still cannot give money directly to a candidate's campaign (hard money), they can now spend unlimited amounts on advertisements that support or attack candidates, provided they do not coordinate directly with the candidate's team. This decision triggered an explosion in political spending and led to the creation of the Super PAC.

Political Action Committees (PACs)

A **Political Action Committee (PAC)** is the financial arm of an interest group. Because corporations and unions are prohibited from giving directly to candidates from their general treasuries, they form PACs to collect voluntary contributions from employees or members. These funds are then distributed to candidates who support the group's interests. Traditional PACs are strictly regulated; they can give no more than 5,000 dollars to a candidate per election. Because they provide a significant portion of the funding for congressional races, they ensure that interest groups have constant access to lawmakers.

The ***Citizens United*** and ***SpeechNow.org v. FEC*** decisions created a new entity: the **Super PAC**. Officially known as "independent expenditure-only committees," Super PACs can raise unlimited sums of money from individuals, corporations, and unions. They cannot give money directly to candidates, but they can spend it on their own to run advertisements or organize ground games. This allows a single billionaire or a major corporation to have a massive influence on an election. In many modern races, the spending by Super PACs exceeds the spending of the candidates themselves.

Feature	Traditional PAC	Super PAC

Contribution Limit	5,000 dollars per candidate	Unlimited
Source of Funds	Individuals only	Individuals, Corps, Unions
Direct Giving	Yes	No
Coordination	Allowed with candidate	Strictly Prohibited

Beyond PACs, the political influence landscape includes **527 groups** and **501(c)(4) organizations**. 527 groups are tax-exempt organizations created primarily to influence elections, but they cannot explicitly say "vote for" or "vote against" a candidate. 501(c)(4) groups are "social welfare" organizations. These are particularly controversial because they are not required to disclose their donors.

This is the source of **dark money** in American politics. A wealthy donor can give ten million dollars to a 501(c)(4), which then gives that money to a Super PAC to run ads. The public sees the Super PAC's name, but they never find out who actually provided the original funding.

The lack of coordination rules is the most difficult part of the law to enforce. While Super PACs and candidates are legally required to remain separate, they often share the same consultants or use “redboxing,” a practice where a candidate puts specific images and talking points on a public website so that a Super PAC knows exactly what content to use in its ads without a private meeting. This bypasses the spirit of the law while technically following its letter. The result is a campaign system where the candidates themselves often have less control over the narrative than the wealthy interests funding the "independent" efforts.

Media and Public Opinion

The final component of political influence is the media, often referred to as the "Fourth Estate." In the American system, the media acts as the primary intermediary between the government and the governed. It provides the information that citizens use to form their opinions and the platform that politicians use to reach the public. The media’s power comes from its ability to engage in **agenda setting**. From choosing which stories to cover and which to ignore, the media determines what the public perceives as the most important issues of the day. If every news outlet leads with a story about a "border crisis," the public will view immigration as the top national priority, regardless of the actual statistics.

The media also influences perception through **framing**. This involves the way a story is presented to the audience. A story about a new tax can be framed as "investing in our future" or as "stealing from hard-working families." These frames guide how the audience interprets the facts. In the modern era of the twenty-four-hour news cycle, the media often prioritizes "horse race journalism” (focusing on who is winning or losing the latest poll) rather than explaining the substantive policy differences between the candidates. This simplifies complex issues into a sporting event, which can lead to a less informed electorate.

The transition from broadcast media to digital media has fundamentally changed the nature of **public opinion**. For decades, most Americans received their news from three major television networks, which provided a relatively centrist, shared set of facts.

Today, the media landscape is fragmented. People can choose to consume news only from sources that reinforce their existing biases. This creates "echo chambers" where citizens are never exposed to opposing viewpoints. Social media algorithms accelerate this process by showing users content that triggers emotional engagement, often leading to the spread of misinformation and radicalization.

Public opinion polling is the tool used to measure these effects. Politicians, interest groups, and the media rely on polls to understand the "will of the people." However, polling is increasingly difficult. Low response rates to phone calls and the difficulty of reaching younger voters make it hard to get a truly representative sample. A poorly worded question can produce a result that doesn't reflect actual belief.

For example, asking "Do you support the government providing healthcare?" will get a different result than asking "Do you support a government takeover of the medical system?"

Public opinion is both a cause and an effect of political influence. Interest groups spend millions of dollars to "shape" public opinion through advertising, hoping that a change in the public mood will force the government to act. At the same time, politicians use polling to "pander" to the public, changing their positions based on the latest data to ensure their reelection. This creates a feedback loop where the line between leadership and following the crowd becomes blurred.

The Aggregation of Influence

The interplay between parties, interest groups, money, and the media creates a political system that is incredibly responsive but often exclusionary. Those with the organization and the resources to navigate this landscape (the “influentials”) have a much louder voice in Washington than the average citizen. This has led to the theory of **Pluralism**, which argues that the competition between many different interest groups ensures that no single group can dominate the government. According to this view, the "clash of interests" eventually produces a policy that reflects the public good.

Critics of pluralism point to **Elite Theory**, which suggests that the system is rigged in favor of a small, wealthy minority. They argue that the high cost of campaigns and the complexity of lobbying ensure that the "interest of the few" almost always outweighs the "interest of the many." They point to the "dark money" and the "revolving door" as evidence that the linkage institutions have been captured by special interests.

A third view, **Hyperpluralism**, suggests that there are now so many interest groups and so many ways to block action that the government has become paralyzed. In this view, every time the government tries to solve a problem, a specific interest group uses its influence to stop it. This leads to gridlock and "policy incoherence," where the government ends up passing contradictory laws to please different groups.

The reality of American governance likely contains elements of all three theories. The system is designed to be difficult to move, requiring a broad consensus among many different actors. While the influence of money and the media is undeniable, the political parties still provide the primary structure for mass participation. The "clash of interests" remains the primary engine of the legislative process.

Understanding this landscape is essential for any citizen who wants to influence the government. It isn't enough to simply vote; one must understand how to navigate the world of PACs, lobbyists, and media narratives. The government responds to those who show up, who organize, and who provide the information and resources it needs to function. In the end, political influence is a form of energy that drives the machinery of the state.

> **Do you believe that the Supreme Court's decision in *Citizens United*, by allowing unlimited corporate and union spending, has fundamentally broken the "pluralist" balance that the Founders intended to protect through a large, extended republic?**

Key Campaign Finance Precedents

Case	Year	Core Ruling	Impact on Modern Politics
Buckley v. Valeo	1976	Money is speech; limits on individual spending unconstitutional.	Allowed wealthy candidates to fund their own campaigns.
McConnell v. FEC	2003	Upheld the ban on soft money.	Forced parties to rely on smaller, disclosed donations.
Citizens United v. FEC	2010	Corps/Unions can spend unlimited independent funds.	Led to the rise of Super PACs and massive outside spending.
McCutcheon v. FEC	2014	Struck down aggregate limits on individual giving.	Allowed a single donor to give to every candidate on a party's ticket.

Chapter 16: Contemporary Challenges to American Governance

The American system of government currently faces a series of stress tests that the Founders likely never envisioned. While the Constitution provides a durable framework, the friction between its 18th-century design and 21st-century political realities has created significant institutional strain. The mechanisms intended to ensure stability and compromise now often produce paralysis. This chapter examines the primary challenges threatening the functionality of the Republic, from the internal collapse of legislative norms to the external pressures of a polarized electorate.

Polarization and Legislative Gridlock

The most visible challenge to modern governance is the rise of extreme **partisan polarization**. In the mid-20th century, the two major parties were loose coalitions with significant ideological overlap. It wasn't uncommon to find liberal Republicans from the Northeast or conservative Democrats from the South. This overlap provided a "middle ground" where bipartisan deals could be struck. Today, that middle ground has largely vanished. The parties have undergone a process of "sorting," where ideological, geographic, and cultural identities have aligned almost perfectly with party labels.

This sorting has led to **affective polarization**, a phenomenon where partisans don't just disagree with the opposing party's policies but view the members of that party as an existential threat to the nation. When voters and politicians perceive the opposition as an enemy rather than a competitor, compromise becomes a form of "treason" to the party base. This environment fundamentally alters how Congress functions. Legislators now face greater pressure from their "flank" in primary elections than from the general electorate in November.

The institutional result of this hostility is **legislative gridlock**. The Senate filibuster, once a rarely used tool for extreme circumstances, has become a routine requirement for nearly all non-budgetary legislation. Because the majority party rarely holds sixty seats, the minority party can block any bill it dislikes. This has effectively turned the Senate into a "60-vote chamber," which stops most major policy initiatives before they can even be debated.

Gridlock has destroyed the "regular order" of the legislative process. Congress now struggles to pass the twelve individual appropriations bills required to fund the government. Instead, it relies on **omnibus spending bills**, which are massive, thousands-of-pages-long documents that are negotiated by a handful of leaders and passed at the last minute to avoid a government shutdown. This process strips rank-and-file members of their ability to amend legislation and prevents the public from understanding what their government is actually doing.

The "Hastert Rule" further complicates House operations. Named after a former Speaker, this informal rule suggests that the Speaker will not bring a bill to the floor unless a "majority of the majority" supports it. In a polarized era, this means that even if a bill has the support of a broad bipartisan majority of the full House, it may never receive a vote if the most ideological wing of the majority party opposes it. The House has moved from a majoritarian body to one governed by the most intense partisans.

Another structural consequence of polarization is the growing reliance on the executive branch to bypass legislative paralysis. When Congress can't act, presidents increasingly turn to executive orders, regulatory agencies, and administrative rulemaking to implement policy.

This can produce short-term results, but it creates instability, as these actions can be reversed by future administrations. Policy becomes cyclical rather than durable, shifting with each election instead of being codified through legislation.

Judicial power expands in parallel. As Congress avoids resolving contentious issues, courts are asked to decide them instead. This places unelected judges at the center of major policy disputes, from healthcare to immigration to election law. Over time, this dynamic reinforces the perception that lasting change comes through litigation rather than legislation, further weakening incentives for compromise within Congress.

Primary elections amplify these trends. In many districts, the general election outcome is effectively predetermined due to geographic and partisan sorting. As a result, the decisive contest occurs in the primary, where turnout is lower and more ideologically intense. Candidates respond by adopting more rigid positions, reducing the space for negotiation once in office. Safe districts produce less electoral accountability for bipartisan cooperation and more reward for partisan loyalty.

Media fragmentation also has a role. Instead of a shared information environment, voters consume news that confirms their existing beliefs. This reinforces partisan identities and reduces exposure to competing viewpoints.

Politicians, in turn, tailor their messaging to segmented audiences, often prioritizing mobilization over persuasion. The feedback loop between media, voters, and elected officials deepens divisions and makes compromise politically costly.

The cumulative effect is a system that remains functional but struggles to address large-scale, long-term challenges. Issues that require sustained coordination, such as fiscal policy, infrastructure, and entitlement reform, are often delayed or handled through temporary measures. While the constitutional framework was designed to slow decision-making, the current level of polarization has shifted that friction from a safeguard into a persistent barrier to governance.

Executive Power Expansion

As Congress has become paralyzed by gridlock, the Presidency has stepped into the vacuum. This trend, often called the rise of the **Imperial Presidency**, involves the steady expansion of executive authority beyond the limits envisioned in Article II. When Congress cannot pass laws to address national problems, Presidents increasingly use **executive orders** and agency rulemaking to implement their agendas unilaterally.

This shift creates a "yo-yo" effect in American policy. Because executive orders can be rescinded by a successor with a stroke of a pen, major national policies on immigration, environmental protection, student loans, and even more minor issues on whether we call the continent's tallest mountain Denali or Mt. McKinley now change every four to eight years based on who occupies the Oval Office. This creates immense instability for the economy and the legal system. It also removes major policy decisions from the reach of the people's representatives in Congress, vesting that power in unelected bureaucrats and a single, powerful executive.

The **Unitary Executive Theory** provides the intellectual justification for much of this expansion. Proponents of this theory argue that because the "executive Power" is vested in a single President, he must have absolute control over the entire executive branch, including independent agencies. This theory challenges the ability of Congress to insulate certain government functions, such as the Department of Justice or the Federal Reserve, from presidential political interference.

Congress is partially to blame for this imbalance. For decades, the legislature has delegated broad, vaguely defined powers to executive agencies. Lawmakers often prefer to pass "goal-oriented" legislation, such as "clean up the air" or "workplace safety," while leaving the difficult, politically risky details to the bureaucracy. While this allows for expert management, it also means that the most significant "laws" governing American life are now written by agency officials rather than elected representatives.

The Supreme Court has recently begun to push back against this delegation through the **Major Questions Doctrine**. This legal principle asserts that if an agency wants to regulate an issue of "vast economic and political significance," it must have clear and specific authorization from Congress. The Court is essentially telling the legislature that it can't shirk its duty to make the most important policy choices for the country. However, until Congress finds a way to overcome its own internal gridlock, the pressure for the President to act alone will likely remain.

Federalism Disputes in the Modern Era

Federalism was designed to be a system of shared power, but in the modern era, it has become a primary arena for partisan combat. As the federal government has become more polarized, states have taken on the role of "resistance" hubs. When the federal government is controlled by one party, states controlled by the other party use their **reserved powers** to challenge national policy or to implement alternative models.

We see this most clearly in the realm of **preemption**. This occurs when federal law overrides state law under the Supremacy Clause. For example, several states have legalized marijuana for recreational use, even though it remains an illegal "Schedule I" substance under the federal Controlled Substances Act. For years, the federal government has largely chosen not to enforce its law in those states, creating a precarious legal gray area where a multi-billion-dollar industry exists in technical violation of federal law.

Immigration has also become a major federalism flashpoint. Some "sanctuary" jurisdictions refuse to cooperate with federal immigration authorities, arguing that doing so would undermine local trust and divert limited police resources.

Conversely, states like Texas have attempted to implement their own border enforcement measures, leading to direct legal standoffs with the Department of Justice over who has the final authority to secure the international boundary.

The 10th Amendment is frequently invoked in these disputes. In the case of *NFIB v. Sebelius* (2012), the Supreme Court ruled that the federal government could not "coerce" states into expanding Medicaid by threatening to pull all of their existing healthcare funding. This reinforced the idea that while the federal government can "encourage" state cooperation with money, it can't treat the states as administrative subdivisions of the national government.

Dispute Category	State Action	Federal Response
Environmental	California sets stricter auto emission standards.	Federal government may grant or deny "waivers" for these rules.
Immigration	States pass laws allowing local police to arrest undocumented migrants.	Federal courts often strike these down as a violation of federal supremacy.
Civil Rights	States pass laws restricting or protecting abortion access post-*Dobbs*.	Federal government uses executive orders or litigation to protect access.

These disputes create a "patchwork" republic where a citizen's fundamental rights and legal obligations can change drastically the moment they cross a state line. While the Founders valued this diversity (the "laboratories of democracy"), the level of divergence today threatens the idea of a single, national marketplace and a unified set of constitutional protections. The Supreme Court is increasingly forced to act as a referee in these high-stakes territorial battles.

Election Administration Controversies

The American election system is uniquely decentralized. There is no single "national election"; instead, there are thousands of local elections coordinated by the states. While this decentralization was originally intended to prevent a central government from rigging the results, it has recently become a source of intense controversy and distrust. The mechanics of how we vote, from registration and mail-in ballots to the certification of results, have become hyper-partisan issues.

The controversy often centers on the tension between **voting access** and **election security**. One camp argues that the primary goal should be to make voting as easy as possible, advocating for expanded mail-in voting, automatic registration, and longer early-voting periods.

They view restrictive laws as a form of modern-day voter suppression. The other camp argues that these measures increase the risk of fraud and undermine public confidence, advocating instead for strict voter ID laws and limits on ballot "harvesting."

The 2020 election and the events of January 6, 2021, exposed a significant weakness in the **Electoral Count Act of 1887**. This old law governed how Congress counts the electoral votes sent by the states. The ambiguity of the law allowed for theories that the Vice President or Congress could unilaterally reject a state's certified results. While Congress recently updated the law to clarify that the Vice President's role is purely ceremonial and to raise the threshold for objecting to results, the underlying distrust in the administration of elections remains a significant threat to the peaceful transfer of power.

The rise of the **Independent State Legislature (ISL)** theory represents a radical challenge to election law. Proponents of this theory argue that the Constitution gives state legislatures the exclusive power to regulate federal elections, meaning that state courts and state constitutions cannot limit their actions. If the Supreme Court were to fully adopt this theory, it would mean that state legislatures could engage in extreme gerrymandering or change election rules without any oversight from their own state's judicial branch. In *Moore v. Harper* (2023), the Court rejected the most extreme version of this theory, but it remains a live topic of debate.

Perhaps the most dangerous challenge is the decline of **institutional trust**. When a significant portion of the electorate believes that the system is "rigged" or that the results are illegitimate, the foundation of a representative republic begins to crumble. This distrust makes it difficult for losers of an election to accept the result, which is the essential prerequisite for a stable democracy. Without a shared set of facts and a common faith in the integrity of the ballot box, the American system of governance cannot survive.

Reform Proposals and Constitutional Debates

The depth of these challenges has prompted a wide range of proposals for structural reform. Some advocates argue that the system is fundamentally broken and requires a "second founding" or a new constitutional convention. Others suggest more targeted statutory changes that could be achieved without the difficult process of a constitutional amendment.

One frequent proposal is the **abolition of the filibuster**. Critics argue that the 60-vote requirement makes it impossible for the winning party to actually govern, leading to the very gridlock and executive overreach discussed earlier. They argue that if a party wins the House, the Senate, and the Presidency, they should be able to pass their agenda and then be held accountable by the voters. Opponents of this change argue that the filibuster is the last remaining check that forces bipartisan compromise and protects the minority from the "tyranny of the majority."

Electoral College reform is another perennial topic. The **National Popular Vote Interstate Compact (NPVIC)** is an attempt to bypass a constitutional amendment. States that join the compact agree to award their electoral votes to the winner of the national popular vote, but only once the participating states collectively hold 270 electoral votes. This would effectively create a direct popular election for President without changing a word of the Constitution. However, it faces massive legal and political hurdles and would likely be challenged in the Supreme Court.

There is also a growing movement for **term limits** for both members of Congress and Supreme Court justices.

For Congress, proponents argue that limits would end the "permanent political class" and bring fresh perspectives to Washington.

For the Supreme Court, some suggest 18-year "staggered" terms so that every president would get to appoint two justices. This would lower the "life-or-death" stakes of every individual vacancy so that the Court more closely reflects the long-term shifts in national opinion.

Other reform ideas include:

- **Ranked Choice Voting (RCV) -** Allowing voters to rank candidates by preference to encourage more moderate, broad-appeal candidates and reduce the power of the two-party duopoly.
- **Independent Redistricting Commissions -** Taking the power to draw congressional lines away from partisan legislatures to end gerrymandering.
- **Expanding the House -** Increasing the number of representatives to reduce the size of districts and make members more responsive to their constituents.
- **Universal Voter Registration -** Making registration automatic for all eligible citizens to increase participation.

The primary obstacle to any of these reforms is **Article V** itself. The process for amending the Constitution is intentionally difficult, requiring two-thirds of both houses of Congress and three-fourths of the states. In a period of high polarization, it's nearly impossible to reach that level of consensus on any significant change. This creates a paradox: the very gridlock and division that make reform necessary also make reform impossible.

The American government is currently in a period of profound transition. The rules and norms that governed the system for much of the 20th century are being discarded in favor of a more aggressive, zero-sum form of politics. Whether the Constitution can adapt to these challenges, or whether it requires a fundamental overhaul, is the central question of modern American life. The "more perfect Union" described in the Preamble is not a destination, but a continuous effort that requires every generation to address the unique threats of their time.

The challenges of the 21st century, from the digital media landscape to the globalized economy, have placed an immense burden on an 18th-century structure. The "checks and balances" intended to prevent tyranny now often prevent any action at all.

As the nation moves forward, the ability of its leaders and its citizens to find a way back to functional compromise will determine whether the American experiment in self-government continues or fades into history.

Given the current level of affective polarization and the structural difficulty of the Article V amendment process, is it more likely that American governance will be reformed through a sudden, major crisis or through the gradual, incremental adoption of state-level changes like ranked choice voting and independent commissions?

Conclusion

You have reached the end of our look through the machinery of American democracy. We started in the heat of a Philadelphia summer in 1787 and ended in the complex, digital, and often divided landscape of today. If you take only one thing away from these pages, let it be this: the United States government isn't a static object that we should take for granted as a permanent institution. History has shown that no government ultimately is, even in the more advanced times that we live in. US government is a living, breathing, and occasionally loud experiment. It was built by people who were deeply skeptical of power, yet they realized that without a functional structure, liberty would quickly vanish into chaos.

The Founders didn't try to write a script for every possible future scenario. They were smart enough to know they couldn't predict the industrial revolution, digital communications, or the rise of a global superpower. Instead, they gave us a framework. They provided the rules of the game and a set of boundaries that no one is supposed to cross. The chapters we looked at showed how these boundaries are constantly tested. Whether it's the President using an executive order to move quickly or the Supreme Court stepping in to redefine a fundamental right, the system is designed for friction.

The Perspective of Time

One of the most important realizations from our look at these core concepts is that the "good old days" of perfect political harmony never actually existed. We often look at the early Republic with a sense of nostalgia, but those years were filled with just as much vitriol and uncertainty as our own. The difference today is the speed at which information travels and the scale of the institutions involved. The core tension remains the same: how do we protect the rights of the individual while still allowing the government to act for the common good?

We often talk about "checks and balances" as a mechanical safety feature. In reality, it's a psychological one. The system works because it assumes that people in power will always want more of it. Giving the House, the Senate, the President, and the Courts the ability to say "no" to each other, the Constitution forces a pause. It forces a conversation. It's designed so that the laws of the land represent something closer to a broad consensus than the temporary whim of a single leader or a narrow majority.

New Perspectives on Old Rules

As we reflect on the material, a few fresh points come to light. We often view the Bill of Rights as a list of things we can do. It's more accurate to see it as a list of things the government *cannot* do to you. This "negative" approach to liberty is the secret to its endurance. It places the burden of proof on the state. If the government wants to limit your speech or search your home, it must justify that action against a clear, written standard. This keeps the power dynamic tilted toward the citizen.

Another point to consider is the shifting nature of federalism. We used to think of the states and the national government as two separate cakes. Today, they're so intermingled that it's almost impossible to find a policy that doesn't involve both. This isn't necessarily a failure of the original design; it's a response to a more connected nation. The "laboratories of democracy" still exist, but they now operate with federal funding and under federal oversight. This creates a system that is incredibly complex but also resilient. If one level of government fails to act on a problem, the other level often steps in to fill the gap.

Your Place in the Machine

The most critical component of this entire structure is the one we started with: "We the People." The government does not run on its own. It requires the constant input, attention, and participation of its citizens. This doesn't just mean voting every four years, although that is the baseline. It means understanding how your local school board operates. It means knowing who represents you in your state capital. It means recognizing that when the system feels broken or unresponsive, the solution is usually more involvement, not less.

Democracy is a high-maintenance form of government. It is slow, it is frustratingly deliberate, and it requires us to live alongside people with whom we deeply disagree. But the alternative, a government where one person or one group makes all the decisions without any check or balance, is exactly what the Americans of 1776 fought to escape. The friction we see in Congress or the debates we hear in the Supreme Court are not signs that the system is failing. They are signs that the system is doing exactly what it was designed to do: prevent the easy exercise of absolute power.

Looking Ahead

The challenges we discussed in the final chapter, from polarization to the expansion of executive reach, are significant. They will require new ideas and perhaps even new laws to address. But the foundation remains strong. The Constitution has survived a Civil War, world wars, economic collapses, and massive social upheavals because it is flexible enough to change but sturdy enough to hold.

You are now equipped with the core concepts of this foundation. You understand why the Senate is different from the House. You know how a bill becomes a law and why the courts have the power to strike it down. You see the hidden influence of interest groups and the persistent reach of the federal bureaucracy. This knowledge is your best defense against misinformation and your best tool for effective citizenship.

Keep asking questions. Keep looking at the primary sources. The experiment continues, and you are one of the researchers. The goal of a "more perfect Union" is a horizon, not a destination. As long as we keep moving toward it, the Republic remains secure.

How has your understanding of the "checks and balances" system changed now that you've seen how often the branches actually cooperate to manage the federal bureaucracy?

Example Answers and Discussion Guide

To what extent did the transition from the "rights of Englishmen" to the "rights of man" fundamentally change the legal arguments used to justify the American Revolution?

The transition shifted the debate from a narrow dispute over the British constitution to a universal claim about human existence. Initially, colonists argued that Parliament violated specific English statutes like the Magna Carta. When they moved to the "rights of man," they adopted John Locke's view that rights come from nature, not from a king. This allowed the revolutionaries to argue that George III didn't just break a law; he violated a moral order that existed before any government. It transformed a local rebellion into a global statement on human liberty.

Was the Great Compromise a necessary practical solution for national survival, or did it create a permanent structural defect by giving disproportionate power to smaller states?

The Great Compromise was an absolute political necessity. Without it, the convention would have dissolved, and the states likely would have formed separate, competing confederacies. However, it did install a lasting imbalance. Today, a voter in a small state has significantly more influence in the Senate than a voter in a large state. While this protects local interests, it frequently allows a minority of the population to block national legislation that the majority supports.

Does the existence of "implied powers" through the Necessary and Proper Clause effectively render the concept of "enumerated powers" obsolete in a modern, complex society?

It hasn't rendered them obsolete, but it has certainly pushed them into the background. The list of eighteen powers in Article I remains the constitutional "anchor," ensuring that the federal government must at least pretend to tie every action to a specific clause. However, the Supreme Court's broad interpretation of what is "necessary" has allowed the government to grow into areas like aviation and digital privacy that the Founders couldn't imagine. If the government had to stick strictly to the literal text, the federal system would have collapsed during the industrial era. Instead, the Elastic Clause serves as a safety valve. It allows the government to function in a modern economy while maintaining the fiction that its authority is still limited to a few specific grants of power. This creates a permanent tension between the literal words on the page and the practical needs of a global superpower.

Do you think the Anti-Federalists' fear that the "Necessary and Proper Clause" would lead to an unlimited expansion of federal power has been proven right by modern American history?

In many ways, the Anti-Federalists were the most accurate prophets of the founding era. They predicted that the combination of the Supremacy Clause and the Elastic Clause would eventually drain the states of their meaningful authority. Today, federal regulations touch almost every aspect of local life, from education standards to the types of lightbulbs you can buy. While the federal government hasn't become a "tyranny" in the traditional sense, it has reached a level of centralization that the Anti-Federalists warned would destroy local self-rule.

Does the modern shift toward "coercive federalism" (where the federal government uses funding to force state compliance) undermine the original intent of the Tenth Amendment as a protection for state sovereignty?

The Tenth Amendment was intended to be a hard barrier, but the power of the purse has turned it into a flexible suggestion. When the federal government offers billions in highway or education funds, it often attaches "strings" that force states to change their laws. While the Supreme Court says this isn't technically "coercion" because states can refuse the money, the reality is that no state can afford to walk away from that revenue.

This practice effectively allows Congress to legislate in areas where it has no direct constitutional authority. If the federal government wants a national drinking age, it doesn't pass a law; it simply threatens to pull highway money from states that don't comply. This has created a "senior-junior" partnership where the states have become administrative agents for national policy. It significantly weakens the idea of states as truly independent sovereigns.

Does the modern trend of "government by executive order" suggest that the legislative branch has become too willing to cede its power to the President, thereby breaking the Madisonian balance?

Yes, it indicates a significant institutional collapse in Congress. Lawmakers often find it easier to let the President make controversial choices through executive orders rather than taking a difficult vote themselves. This protects their reelection chances but leaves the nation's policy to the whims of the current occupant of the White House. It replaces permanent law with temporary decrees, which is exactly the kind of concentrated power the Founders feared.

Do you believe the 17th Amendment, by shifting the election of senators from state legislatures to the people, fundamentally weakened the principle of federalism by removing the states' direct voice in the national government?

The 17th Amendment fundamentally altered the Senate's identity. Before 1913, senators acted as ambassadors for their state governments, ensuring that federal laws didn't infringe on state authority. Today, senators answer to the same popular passions as representatives. This move increased democracy but decreased the institutional protection for the states. Without a direct representative in Washington, state governments lost their most significant check on federal expansion.

In your view, would the introduction of multi-member districts with proportional representation be a more effective way to reduce the impact of gerrymandering than the current reliance on independent redistricting commissions?

Independent commissions merely attempt to draw fairer lines for a system that is inherently prone to manipulation. As long as you have "winner-take-all" districts, the majority party will find ways to marginalize the minority. Multi-member districts would change the fundamental math of the election. Under such a system, if a party wins forty percent of the vote in a large district, they would receive forty percent of the seats.

This approach would make gerrymandering almost impossible because the lines wouldn't matter nearly as much as the total vote count. It would also encourage the growth of third parties and force the major parties to appeal to a broader audience. While it would require a significant shift in American political culture, it offers a structural solution to a problem that independent commissions only address at the surface level. It would move the focus from geography to ideology.

Does the modern trend toward "top-down" leadership, where major bills are negotiated by a few leaders rather than through the traditional committee process, undermine the benefits of specialization that the committee system was designed to provide?

It certainly degrades the quality of the legislation. The committee system was designed to ensure that experts in agriculture or defense had the first word on those topics. When the Speaker or the Majority Leader skips this process to negotiate a "mega-bill" behind closed doors, they often overlook technical details and unintended consequences. This centralized power prioritizes partisan wins over sound policy making.

Given the frequency of "silent filibusters" and the requirement for 60 votes in the Senate, has the legislative process become so difficult that it now favors stagnation over the "more perfect Union" promised in the Preamble?

Stagnation has become the default setting of the Senate. While the Founders wanted a slow process, they didn't intend for a permanent minority to block nearly all major action. When the government can't pass a budget or address national crises because of a 60-vote threshold, the "blessings of liberty" are hard to secure. It creates a vacuum that the President usually fills with unilateral action.

Do you believe the increasing use of the "Authorization for Use of Military Force" (AUMF) as a substitute for a formal declaration of war has permanently shifted the balance of power toward the executive branch?

The shift appears permanent. By passing broad, open-ended authorizations, Congress has essentially given the President a "blank check" to wage war across different countries and decades. A formal declaration of war requires a specific target and a clear end goal. An AUMF allows for "forever wars" where the executive branch decides the scope and duration of hostilities. It has turned the Commander in Chief into the sole decider of when the nation is at war, which is the exact concentration of power the Framers tried to prevent by giving the power of the sword to the legislature.

Do you think the "major questions doctrine" is an essential tool for reasserting congressional authority, or does it prevent the executive branch from effectively responding to modern crises that the Founders couldn't have envisioned?

The "major questions doctrine" acts as a necessary "reset button" for a government that has become too dependent on bureaucrats. For decades, executive agencies have used vague, fifty-year-old laws to claim massive new powers over the economy and social life. The Supreme Court is now telling these agencies that if they want to make a huge change, they must go back to Congress and get a specific new law.

While this can slow down the response to a crisis, it ensures that the most important decisions are made by people who are actually accountable to the voters. It forces Congress to stop "punting" its responsibilities to the executive branch. If a crisis is truly national, then the representatives of the people should be the ones to debate and authorize the solution. Without this doctrine, the administrative state would eventually become a government unto itself, operating entirely outside the reach of the democratic process.

Do you believe that life tenure for federal judges is still the best way to ensure judicial independence, or has it led to a system where the stakes of every appointment are too high for a healthy democracy?

Life tenure succeeds in keeping judges independent, but it has turned the Supreme Court into a political battlefield. Because a single appointment can last forty years, the confirmation process has become a zero-sum war. The result is a court that often feels like a third legislative chamber rather than a neutral arbiter of law. Introducing term limits might lower the temperature of these battles while still providing enough time for independence.

Does the modern shift toward "originalism" in the Supreme Court threaten to roll back the decades of progress made in expanding civil rights through the "living constitution" interpretation of the Fourteenth Amendment?

It presents a significant challenge to many established precedents. Originalists argue that if a right (like the right to privacy or marriage equality) isn't mentioned in the text and wasn't part of the public understanding in 1868, it isn't a constitutional right. This creates a conflict with a "living constitution" approach that views the 14th Amendment as a broad promise of evolving equality. The debate is essentially over whether we should be governed by the past or the present.

Do you believe that the Supreme Court's decision in *Citizens United*, by allowing unlimited corporate and union spending, has fundamentally broken the "pluralist" balance that the Founders intended to protect through a large, extended republic?

The decision has certainly tilted the balance in a way that Madison didn't anticipate. Madison's theory of pluralism relied on a vast number of small, competing interests that would naturally cancel each other out. He didn't imagine a world where a single corporation or a handful of billionaires could spend more than the combined contributions of millions of regular citizens.

When a few "super-interests" have the financial power to dominate the media and the airwaves, the "clash of factions" is no longer a fair fight. It allows those with the most money to set the national agenda and frame the debate before the average voter even hears the facts. While the Court views this as protected speech, critics argue it has turned the republic into an "oligarchy" where the government only listens to the highest bidder. It hasn't completely broken the system, but it has certainly made it much harder for a broad, diverse coalition of regular citizens to compete for influence.

Given the current level of affective polarization and the structural difficulty of the Article V amendment process, is it more likely that American governance will be reformed through a sudden, major crisis or through the gradual, incremental adoption of state-level changes like ranked choice voting and independent commissions?

History suggests that major structural changes to the Constitution almost always follow a significant national trauma, such as the Civil War or the Great Depression. However, the current "gridlock" at the national level makes the state-level path more practical in the short term. As more states adopt ranked choice voting and independent commissions, they create a "proof of concept" that can eventually pressure the federal government to change its own rules. Reform will likely be a slow, bottom-up process until a major crisis forces a national "reset."

Terms & Definitions

- **House of Burgesses** - This assembly established the first representative governing body in the American colonies. It allowed Virginia landowners to pass local laws and set a precedent for self-governance.
- **Mayflower Compact** - This document represents an early social contract among settlers to form a civil government and obey its laws. It established that a government's legitimacy comes from the consent of the people it rules.
- **Salutary Neglect** - This unofficial British policy involved the intentional lack of enforcement of parliamentary laws in the American colonies. It permitted the colonies to develop their own independent political and economic systems for decades.
- **English Common Law** - This legal system relies on judicial precedents and customs rather than written statutes alone. It forms the basis of the American judiciary and emphasizes consistency across past court rulings.
- **Magna Carta** - This 1215 charter established the principle that the monarch is not above the law. It introduced early protections for due process and limited the arbitrary power of the state.
- **Due Process** - This constitutional guarantee ensures that the government follows fair and established legal procedures before depriving someone of life, liberty, or property. It protects individuals from arbitrary state actions in both criminal and civil matters.
- **Natural Rights** - these are fundamental freedoms that every person possesses from birth, such as life, liberty, and property. Philosophers like John Locke argued that these rights aren't granted by governments and can't be taken away.
- **Social Contract** - This theory describes an agreement where people give up some individual freedoms in exchange for state protection of their remaining rights. If the government violates this agreement, the people possess the right to change or abolish it.
- **Popular Sovereignty** - This principle asserts that the ultimate authority of a government comes from the people. The phrase "We the People" in the Constitution's Preamble serves as its most direct expression.
- **Separation of Powers** - This structural design divides government authority into three distinct branches to prevent any single person or group from gaining absolute control. It assigns the power to make, enforce, and interpret laws to different bodies.
- **Articles of Confederation** - This document served as the first constitution of the United States and created a weak central government that lacked the power to tax. It established a league of friendship among sovereign states rather than a unified nation.
- **Shays' Rebellion** - This armed uprising by debt-ridden farmers in Massachusetts exposed the fatal weaknesses of the Articles of Confederation. It convinced many national leaders that the country needed a stronger central authority to maintain order.
- **Virginia Plan** - This proposal at the Constitutional Convention favored large states by suggesting a bicameral legislature with representation based

on population. It called for a strong national government with three branches.

- **New Jersey Plan** - This proposal favored small states by suggesting a unicameral legislature where every state received exactly one vote. It aimed to preserve state sovereignty while granting Congress limited powers to tax and regulate trade.
- **Great Compromise** - This agreement settled the debate over representation by creating a bicameral legislature. It established a House of Representatives based on population and a Senate where every state has equal standing.
- **Three-Fifths Compromise** - This political deal allowed Southern states to count sixty percent of their enslaved population for both representation and taxation. It embedded the institution of slavery into the initial political balance of the new government.
- **Electoral College** - This system selects the President through electors appointed by each state rather than a direct popular vote. It balances the influence of large and small states in the executive selection process.
- **Federalists** - these supporters of the new Constitution argued that a strong central government was necessary for national survival and economic stability. They authored many essays to persuade the public to support ratification.
- **Anti-Federalists** - these critics of the Constitution feared that a central government would become tyrannical and destroy state sovereignty. They demanded a Bill of Rights to protect individual liberties from federal overreach.
- **Federalist Papers** - This collection of eighty-five essays explained the logic of the Constitution and defended its specific provisions. James Madison, Alexander Hamilton, and John Jay wrote them to influence the New York ratifying convention.
- **Bill of Rights** - these first ten amendments to the Constitution list specific protections for individual liberties and rights. They were added to satisfy the demands of critics who feared the new government's reach.
- **Ratification** - This formal approval process required nine of the thirteen states to accept the Constitution before it could take effect. It involved special conventions elected by the people rather than existing state legislatures.
- **Tenth Amendment** - This provision clarifies that powers not delegated to the federal government belong to the states or the people. It serves as the primary constitutional protection for state sovereignty.
- **Enumerated Powers** - these specific authorities are explicitly listed in Article I, Section 8 of the Constitution, such as the power to coin money or declare war. They define the legal boundaries of federal activity.
- **Implied Powers** - these authorities aren't explicitly written in the Constitution but are logically derived from those that are. They allow the federal government to address modern issues through the Necessary and Proper Clause.
- **Necessary and Proper Clause** - This provision allows Congress to make laws essential for carrying out its listed powers. It's often called the Elastic Clause because it permits the reach of federal authority to expand.
- **Supremacy Clause** - This article establishes the Constitution and federal laws as the highest law of the land. It ensures that valid national laws override conflicting state regulations.

- **Federalism** - This system divides sovereignty between a national government and several regional state governments. It allows both levels to operate directly on the citizens within their respective jurisdictions.
- **Dual Federalism** - This model views the federal and state governments as separate entities with clearly defined spheres of authority. Political scientists often compare this arrangement to a layer cake.
- **Cooperative Federalism** - This model involves the intermingling of federal and state responsibilities to solve complex national problems. It relies on shared funding and joint administration of programs, resembling a marble cake.
- **Fiscal Federalism** - This pattern of spending, taxing, and providing grants defines the modern relationship between the national and state governments. It uses the federal government's massive revenue to influence state-level policies.
- **Categorical Grant** - This federal funding must be used for a specific, narrowly defined purpose, such as school lunch programs. It often comes with strict federal rules that states must follow to receive the money.
- **Block Grant** - This federal funding provides states with significant flexibility in how they spend money within a broad functional area, such as community development. It allows states to tailor programs to their specific local needs.
- **Unfunded Mandate** - This federal requirement forces states to perform specific actions without providing the money to pay for them. These laws often create significant financial strain for state and local governments.
- **Devolution** - This political movement aims to return power and responsibility from the federal government to the state governments. It often involves turning centralized federal programs into block grants.
- **Checks and Balances** - This system allows each branch of government to monitor and limit the actions of the other two branches. It ensures that no single part of the government can act without the consent or review of the others.
- **Veto** - This executive power allows the President to reject a bill passed by Congress. It forces the legislature to either abandon the bill or find enough support to override the objection.
- **Pocket Veto** - This occurs when a President ignores a bill and Congress adjourns within ten days of its passage. Because Congress is no longer in session, the bill dies and can't be overridden.
- **Veto Override** - This legislative action allows Congress to pass a bill into law despite a presidential veto. It requires a two-thirds majority vote in both the House of Representatives and the Senate.
- **Judicial Review** - This power allows the courts to declare acts of Congress or actions of the President unconstitutional. It makes the judicial branch the final arbiter of what the Constitution means.
- **Marbury v. Madison** - This 1803 Supreme Court case established the principle of judicial review. It affirmed that the Constitution is the supreme law and that courts possess the duty to strike down conflicting statutes.
- **Impeachment** - This formal process allows the House of Representatives to charge a federal official with serious misconduct. It serves as the first step toward removing an official from office through a Senate trial.
- **Advice and Consent** - This Senate authority involves reviewing and approving presidential appointments and treaties. It acts as a primary check on the executive branch's ability to fill the government or enter international pacts.

- **Bicameralism** - This term describes a legislature consisting of two separate houses or chambers. In the United States, it provides an internal check by requiring both the House and Senate to agree on every law.
- **Reapportionment** - This reallocation of House seats occurs every ten years following the results of the national census. It triggers shifts in political influence as seats move from slow-growing states to fast-growing ones.
- **Redistricting** - This process involves redrawing the boundaries of congressional districts within a state. It usually happens after reapportionment to ensure that each district contains roughly the same number of people.
- **Gerrymandering** - This practice involves drawing district lines to favor a specific political party or incumbent. It often results in oddly shaped districts that dilute the voting power of the opposition.
- **Single-Member District** - This electoral system awards one seat in a legislature to the candidate who receives the most votes in a specific geographic area. It discourages third parties and strengthens the two-party system.
- **Speaker of the House** - This presiding officer of the House of Representatives holds significant control over the legislative agenda. The majority party chooses this leader, who stands second in the line of presidential succession.
- **Majority Leader** - This party official manages the daily legislative schedule and serves as the primary spokesperson for the majority party in their chamber. They work closely with other leaders to advance their party's goals.
- **Minority Leader** - This official leads the opposition party in the House or Senate and works to maintain party unity. They focus on offering alternative policy visions and preparing for the next election.
- **Whip** - This party leader's job is to count votes before they happen and ensure that members show up to vote in alignment with leadership. They act as the primary communication link between the party leaders and the rank-and-file members.
- **President Pro Tempore** - This Senate official presides over the chamber in the absence of the Vice President. The position usually goes to the most senior member of the majority party.
- **Standing Committee** - This permanent legislative body handles bills in a specific policy area, such as agriculture or foreign affairs. Most of the actual work of drafting and refining laws happens within these committees.
- **Select Committee** - This temporary body is created for a specific purpose, such as conducting a one-time investigation or studying a new issue. They usually don't possess the authority to propose legislation to the full chamber.
- **Joint Committee** - This group includes members from both the House and the Senate and focuses on administrative matters or long-term studies. They help coordinate non-legislative activities between the two chambers.
- **Conference Committee** - This temporary joint committee reconciles the differences between House and Senate versions of the same bill. It ensures that a piece of legislation is identical before it's sent to the President.
- **Rules Committee** - This House body determines the terms for debating a bill, including how much time is allowed and which amendments can be offered. It serves as a vital gatekeeper for the majority party's agenda.

- **Markup** - This process involves committee members going through a bill line by line to propose amendments and rewrite sections. It's the stage where the specific details of a law are finalized.
- **Filibuster** - This Senate tactic involves using long speeches or procedural delays to prevent a vote on a bill. It effectively requires a super-majority of sixty votes to pass most major legislation.
- **Cloture** - This Senate procedure allows the chamber to end a filibuster and move to a final vote. It requires the support of three-fifths of the full Senate, currently sixty votes.
- **Discharge Petition** - This House maneuver allows a majority of members to force a bill out of a reluctant committee. It's a rare and difficult process used to bypass committee chairs who refuse to act on popular legislation.
- **Rider** - This provision is added to a bill that has nothing to do with the bill's main topic. Senators frequently use them to pass controversial items by attaching them to popular or necessary legislation.
- **Power of the Purse** - This constitutional authority gives Congress the exclusive right to authorize the spending of federal money. It acts as the primary check on the executive branch's ability to operate.
- **Appropriation** - This legislative act provides a specific amount of money to a federal agency or program for a single fiscal year. It's the second step in the funding process after a program has been authorized.
- **Authorization** - This legislative act creates or continues a federal program and sets a ceiling for its funding. It establishes the legal framework for the program but doesn't actually provide the money.
- **Oversight** - This congressional function involves monitoring and supervising the executive branch's implementation of laws. It ensures that agencies spend money efficiently and follow the intent of the legislature.
- **Casework** - This involves members of Congress helping their constituents navigate the federal bureaucracy. It builds personal loyalty and serves as a direct link between citizens and their government.
- **Executive Order** - This formal directive from the President manages the operations of federal agencies and possesses the force of law. It's a primary mechanism for the executive branch to act without direct congressional approval.
- **Executive Agreement** - This pact between the President and the head of a foreign government doesn't require Senate approval. It allows the executive to move quickly on international matters but lacks the legal permanence of a treaty.
- **Federal Bureaucracy** - This massive network of agencies and employees performs the daily work of the federal government. It's organized into departments and commissions that implement the laws passed by Congress.
- **Cabinet** - This group of advisors consists of the heads of the fifteen executive departments. They help the President manage the federal government and develop national policy.
- **Rulemaking** - This administrative process allows executive agencies to create specific regulations that carry the force of law. It involves public notice and comment periods to ensure transparency.
- **Independent Regulatory Commission** - This agency is designed to be insulated from political pressure while regulating specific parts of the economy. Its leaders serve fixed terms and can't be fired by the President without just cause.
- **Merit System** - This civil service practice hires and promotes federal employees based on their qualifications and performance rather than

political loyalty. It replaced the older spoils system that rewarded political supporters with government jobs.

- **Original Jurisdiction** - This describes a court's authority to hear a case for the first time. The Supreme Court possesses this power for cases involving ambassadors or disputes between states.
- **Appellate Jurisdiction** - This describes a court's authority to review decisions made by lower courts. The vast majority of the Supreme Court's workload involves this type of review.
- **Writ of Certiorari** - This formal order from the Supreme Court directs a lower court to send up the records of a case for review. It's the primary way the Court selects the few cases it will hear each year.
- **Stare Decisis** - This legal principle encourages judges to follow past court rulings when deciding similar current cases. it ensures that the law remains predictable and stable over time.
- **Precedent** - This is a court decision that serves as a guide for future cases involving similar legal questions. Lower courts are generally required to follow the precedents set by higher courts.
- **Originalism** - This judicial philosophy argues that the Constitution should be interpreted according to its original public meaning at the time it was adopted. It rejects the idea that judges should adapt the text to modern social values.
- **Civil Liberties** - these are individual freedoms that the Constitution protects from government interference, such as freedom of speech. They act as limits on what the government can legally do to its citizens.
- **Civil Rights** - these are government protections against discrimination based on characteristics like race or gender. They ensure that all citizens receive equal treatment under the law.
- **Establishment Clause** - This First Amendment provision prohibits the government from creating an official religion or favoring one faith over another. It aims to maintain a neutral public square regarding religious matters.
- **Free Exercise Clause** - This provision protects a citizen's right to practice their religion as they see fit. It prevents the government from interfering with religious beliefs and many religious practices.
- **Equal Protection Clause** - This Fourteenth Amendment provision mandates that states treat all citizens equally under the law. It has served as the primary legal mechanism for dismantling segregation and fighting discrimination.
- **Selective Incorporation** - This judicial process applies most of the protections in the Bill of Rights to state governments through the Fourteenth Amendment. It ensures that fundamental liberties are protected at both the state and federal levels.
- **Lobbying** - This practice involves professional advocates attempting to influence the decisions of government officials. It provides legislators with specialized information but often raises concerns about the influence of wealthy interests.
- **Political Action Committee (PAC)** - This organization collects voluntary contributions from members to donate to political candidates. It allows interest groups to participate legally in the campaign finance system.
- **Super PAC** - This type of committee can raise and spend unlimited sums of money to support or attack candidates independently. They are prohibited from coordinating their activities directly with the candidates they support.

Summary of Each Amendment

1st Amendment – Protects freedom of religion, speech, press, assembly, and petition. It creates the baseline for open debate and dissent, allowing citizens to criticize government, organize politically, and exchange ideas without fear of punishment. Without it, democratic accountability collapses quickly.

2nd Amendment – Recognizes the right to keep and bear arms. Historically tied to militias, modern interpretation focuses on individual ownership, with ongoing debates over regulation and public safety.

3rd Amendment – Bars forced quartering of soldiers in private homes. Rarely invoked today.

4th Amendment – Protects against unreasonable searches and seizures, requiring warrants based on probable cause. Its importance has expanded in the digital era, where courts must determine how these protections apply to phones, data, and surveillance technologies that didn't exist at the founding.

5th Amendment – Provides core legal protections: no self-incrimination, no double jeopardy, due process, and compensation for government takings of private property.

6th Amendment – Guarantees a fair criminal trial: speedy, public, impartial jury, legal counsel, and the right to confront witnesses. It defines procedural justice in courtrooms.

7th Amendment – Preserves jury trials in civil cases involving monetary disputes, reinforcing citizen participation in the legal system beyond criminal law.

8th Amendment – Prohibits excessive bail, excessive fines, and cruel and unusual punishment, shaping debates over sentencing, incarceration conditions, and capital punishment.

9th Amendment – Makes clear that rights exist beyond those listed in the Constitution, preventing a narrow reading of individual liberty.

10th Amendment – Reserves undelegated powers to the states or the people, anchoring federalism and limiting centralized authority.

11th Amendment – Limits lawsuits against states in federal court, reinforcing state sovereign immunity.

12th Amendment – Fixes flaws in the Electoral College by separating votes for president and vice president.

13th Amendment – Abolishes slavery and involuntary servitude, except as punishment for a crime. It marks a foundational shift in American law and society, redefining freedom at the constitutional level.

14th Amendment – Establishes citizenship, due process, and equal protection under the law. It is the backbone of modern civil rights, used to apply most of the Bill of Rights to the states and to challenge discriminatory laws across decades.

15th Amendment – Prohibits denying the vote based on race. Enforcement required later civil rights laws.

16th Amendment – Authorizes a federal income tax, dramatically expanding national revenue capacity.

17th Amendment – Creates direct election of senators, increasing democratic accountability.

18th Amendment – Established Prohibition, banning alcohol nationwide. It triggered black markets and enforcement challenges, ultimately proving difficult to sustain politically and socially.

19th Amendment – Grants women the right to vote, expanding democratic participation after decades of organized activism and political pressure.

20th Amendment – Adjusts start dates for elected officials, reducing transition delays.

21st Amendment – Repeals Prohibition, returning alcohol regulation to states.

22nd Amendment – Limits presidents to two terms, preventing long-term consolidation of executive power and formalizing an unwritten precedent.

23rd Amendment – Gives Washington, D.C. electoral votes in presidential elections.

24th Amendment – Eliminates poll taxes in federal elections, removing a financial barrier used to suppress voter turnout, particularly among poorer citizens in certain regions.

25th Amendment – Clarifies presidential succession and disability procedures, giving continuity of leadership during crises or incapacity.

26th Amendment – Lowers voting age to 18, aligning political rights with military service obligations.

27th Amendment – Delays congressional pay raises until after the next election, adding a layer of accountability by giving voters a chance to respond before changes take effect.

References & Recommended Readings

Amar, A. R. (2005). *America's Constitution: A Biography*. Random House.

Breyer, S. (2005). *Active Liberty: Interpreting Our Democratic Constitution*. Knopf.

Caro, R. A. (2002). *The Years of Lyndon Johnson: Master of the Senate*. Alfred A. Knopf.

Chernow, R. (2004). *Alexander Hamilton*. Penguin Press.

Dahl, R. A. (2003). *How Democratic Is the American Constitution?* Yale University Press.

Ellis, J. J. (2000). *Founding Brothers: The Revolutionary Generation*. Alfred A. Knopf.

Fenno, R. F. (1978). *Home Style: House Members in Their Districts*. Little, Brown.

Fiorina, M. P. (2011). *Culture War? The Myth of a Polarized America*. Pearson Longman.

Hamilton, A., Madison, J., & Jay, J. (1788). *The Federalist Papers*. (C. Rossiter, Ed.). New American Library.

Hamilton, L. H. (2004). *How Congress Works and Why You Should Care*. Indiana University Press.

Hobbes, T. (1651). *Leviathan*. (R. Tuck, Ed.). Cambridge University Press.

Irons, P. (2006). *A People's History of the Supreme Court*. Penguin Books.

Jefferson, T. (1776). *The Declaration of Independence*. National Archives.

Keyssar, A. (2000). *The Right to Vote: The Contested History of Democracy in the United States*. Basic Books.

Locke, J. (1689). *Two Treatises of Government*. (P. Laslett, Ed.). Cambridge University Press.

Madison, J. (1787). *Notes of Debates in the Federal Convention of 1787*. (A. Koch, Ed.). Ohio University Press.

Mann, T. E., & Ornstein, N. J. (2012). *It's Even Worse Than It Looks: How the American Constitutional System Collided with the New Politics of Extremism*. Basic Books.

Mayhew, D. R. (2004). *Congress: The Electoral Connection*. Yale University Press.

Montesquieu, C. de S. (1748). *The Spirit of the Laws*. (A. M. Cohler, B. C. Miller, & H. S. Stone, Eds.). Cambridge University Press.

Neustadt, R. E. (1990). *Presidential Power and the Modern Presidents: The Politics of Leadership from Roosevelt to Reagan*. Free Press.

Oleszek, W. J. (2014). *Congressional Procedures and the Policy Process*. CQ Press.

Rakove, J. N. (1996). *Original Meanings: Politics and Ideas in the Making of the Constitution*. Alfred A. Knopf.

Rousseau, J. J. (1762). *The Social Contract*. (M. Cranston, Trans.). Penguin Books.

Sabato, L. J. (2007). *A More Perfect Constitution: 23 Proposals to Revitalize Our Constitution and Make America a Fairer Country*. Walker & Company.

Scalia, A. (1997). *A Matter of Interpretation: Federal Courts and the Law*. Princeton University Press.

Schattschneider, E. E. (1960). *The Semisovereign People: A Realist's View of Democracy in America*. Holt, Rinehart and Winston.

Sinclair, B. (2012). *Unorthodox Lawmaking: New Legislative Processes in the U.S. Congress*. CQ Press.

Sunstein, C. R. (2001). *Republic.com*. Princeton University Press.

Tocqueville, A. de. (1835). *Democracy in America*. (H. C. Mansfield & D. Winthrop, Trans.). University of Chicago Press.

Wood, G. S. (1969). *The Creation of the American Republic, 1776-1787*. University of North Carolina Press.

Recommended Readings

Beeman, R. (2009). *Plain, Honest Men: The Making of the American Constitution*. Random House.

This text recreates the daily friction of the Philadelphia convention to show how the delegates negotiated their core differences. It shows how compromise, personality clashes, and strategic concessions shaped the final Constitution more than abstract theory alone.

Epstein, L., & Walker, T. G. (2020). *Constitutional Law for a Changing America: Rights, Liberties, and Justice*. CQ Press.

This book analyzes how the Supreme Court's interpretation of civil liberties has evolved through landmark judicial rulings over time. It also connects these rulings to broader political and social shifts, showing how constitutional meaning adapts to changing national priorities.

Kernell, S. (2006). *Going Public: New Strategies of Presidential Leadership*. CQ Press.

The author explains how presidents bypass the legislative branch to build direct public support for their specific policy agendas.

Levitsky, S., & Ziblatt, D. (2018). *How Democracies Die*. Crown.

This study identifies the informal norms and institutional guards that prevent the collapse of republican systems in the face of polarization.

Prior, M. (2007). *Post-Broadcast Democracy: How Media Choice Increases Inequality in Political Involvement and Polarizes Elections*. Cambridge University Press.

This work details how the fragmenting media landscape increases partisan division by allowing voters to avoid opposing viewpoints entirely. It also shows how algorithmic curation reinforces existing beliefs by prioritizing emotionally engaging, like-minded content. Over time, this reduces shared factual baselines, making consensus and compromise more difficult in both public opinion and policymaking.

Wilson, J. Q. (1989). *Bureaucracy: What Government Agencies Do and Why They Do It*. Basic Books.

This analysis explains the internal logic and administrative constraints that define how federal agencies implement national law.

www.ingramcontent.com/pod-product-compliance
Lightning Source LLC
LaVergne TN
LVHW010623100826
845148LV00014B/3085

9798900420752